Heavenly Sunshine

Heavenly

Letters To The

Compiled by

Sunshine

"Old-Fashioned Revival Hour"

11760

Mrs. Charles E. Fuller

FLEMING H. REVELL COMPANY

The letters contained in this little book have already been a blessing to many hearts. I hereby give them to the public in this permanent form as a tribute to my beloved husband, Charles E. Fuller, with a profound sense of gratitude to Almighty God who in His most gracious providence has permitted me to make life's brief pilgrimage toward the heavenly City in the loving companionship of such a good man.

Grace Payton Fuller

INTRODUCTION

Of the many letters received through the years in response to the Old-Fashioned Revival Hour broadcast, all are answered when it is possible and feasible to do so. A few of special appeal are chosen each week by Mrs. Charles E. Fuller, the first lady of the Revival Hour, to be read to the international radio audience. Considering that audience as a great congregation gathered for worship, we might say that "letter-time" on the Hour is, as it were, the time of testimony, when the brethren, speaking through Mrs. Fuller, bear a witness to what the Lord has done for them. Of these "testimonies" a choice selection of the most interesting and edifying has been made for this little volume.

No sort of literature is more personal and therefore more captivating than the letter. It may seem a modest form beside the epic or the novel, but we should never forget that the New Testament itself is made up of letters, some to young churches, some to individuals—as Paul's letter to Philemon—and all of them highly personal. For that reason we know more about Paul than any other man in the apostolic age. There is, then, the highest propriety in the time-honored custom of publishing correspondence.

This particular collection, however, can hardly justify itself at the bar of custom, for the letters herein contained were not penned by great men, nor inspired by profound minds. They cannot boast even the excellence of literary beauty; their charm and power lie in another dimension. Coming from men and women in many lands and many stations of life, they reveal the spectrum of the human heart in its conflict with sin and contact with God. To read them is an education; to understand them, a foretaste of glory.

Heavenly Sunshine

For God, who commanded the light to shine out of darkness, hath shined in our hearts, to give the light of the knowledge of the glory of God in the face of Jesus Christ (II Corinthians 4:6).

To explain the title of our little book to those who have listened to the Old-Fashioned Revival Hour, would be as superfluous as the following excerpt is interesting. A young missionary in India writing to her parents relates:

Dear Folks,

On my last medical safari into an unreached area, I was on trek through thick bush when I came upon a clear stream and decided to sit a while and rest. While drinking in the beauty of our Father's great creation, I heard a little voice off in the hills singing, "Heavenly Sunshine," in Kikamba. As I traced it down, I

11

found a little fellow tending goats, singing at the top of his lungs, and the look on that black face with pearly white teeth, showed deep joy. This was a lad who attended Sunday school at the Mission, and had accepted Christ as Saviour, walking twelve miles each Sunday to learn more of his Saviour—rain or shine.

Here is an interesting letter from North Dakota.

Dear Rev. Fuller,

A few months ago one of our sailor boys returned from Africa, and he was telling us about the poverty-stricken native children that surrounded their boat at a certain African port, begging for money. The sailors would ask them to sing for them, before throwing coins for them to dive after, which the children did; and what do you suppose some of those African children sang—"Heavenly Sunshine!" Where did they learn it? Why, through hearing your program!

From North Wales a man writes:

Dear Dr. Fuller,

Your program comes in clearly here and I enjoy every minute of it. Your song, "Heavenly Sunshine," has become very popular, too.

When I was on a holiday in London a few months ago, I was in a railroad station and surprised to hear someone in the crowd whistling "Heavenly Sunshine." I went to investigate and found an elderly man whistling away happily. We had a chat and I found he had come from Italy for the festival of Britain. He was a Christian, like me, and has been hearing you at home in Italy, and he, too, loves that chorus.

I hear that they also sing it in the Irish lanes, and out on the Scottish moors, when the rain is falling and the wind is howling. "Heavenly Sunshine" means so much all around the world now, Brother Fuller.

Whether or not "Heavenly Sunshine" is sung in the Irish lanes, as our Welsh friend has heard, we do know that it has been sung on the main streets of Dublin. Miss Eva Stuart Watt, reporting in the *Sunday School Times* some time ago, observes:

Thousands of Irish Catholics are listening to messages over the air from Radio Luxemburg and Monte Carlo. Dr. Fuller of the Old-Fashioned Revival Hour is becoming known almost nationwide.

A week or two ago four young Christians were holding an open-air meeting in Dublin's city center. When the listeners numbered about two hundred, a girl playing a piano-accordion said to the crowd, "We are now going to sing 'Heavenly Sunshine,' and I want you all to join in." And they did! Imagine one of the main thoroughfares of a city like Dublin resounding with a song from Roman Catholic lips, "Heavenly sunshine! Heavenly sunshine! Hallelujah! Jesus is mine," and that toward the end of the Marian Year, when every attempt has been made to focus the people's attention on "Mary the Mother of God" as mediatrix between God and man and co-redeemer with Christ for the world. Obviously the words had already become familiar through the radio.

A Roman Catholic servant in an Irish country mansion recently asked the daughter of the household if she liked to listen to the radio. "I do," she replied. "Well, I hope ye'll turn it on of a Thursday night at 11 o'clock," he rejoined, "and ye'll hear, miss, what I call real Christianity." (i.e. The Old-Fashioned

Revival Hour heard in Britain from Luxemburg.)

Though the Hebrews did not worship the sun, the Psalmist celebrates the glories of that bright luminary in the familiar words, "His going forth is from the end of the heaven, and his circuit unto the end of it; and there is nothing hid from the heat thereof" (Psalm 19:6). In like manner, the "heavenly sunshine" of the gospel has, through the ministry of the Old-Fashioned Revival Hour, shed its benign rays over many lands, as the following letters testify.

Dear Brother Fuller,
I am a sailor on a British ship, and during my years of traveling around this old world, in almost every port I have picked up the Old-Fashioned Revival Hour. The first time was at home in Scotland. Back in the old country many tune in to the Luxemburg station, and I personally know that many from Petershead, in the north of Scotland, right down to the very south of England, never miss hearing you. Over in Europe, too, I've picked up your broadcast in many ports, radiating out from the powerful transmitter of Luxemburg

as far south as the Mediterranean Sea, as we headed for Egypt and the Suez Canal. Then, once we get clear of Aden and the Red Sea, going down the Indian Ocean, I've picked you up coming from Ceylon. This station is also very powerful and can be heard from South Africa right over to the Australian coast. In the Pacific, Manila is so powerful that I have found you all around China, Japan, and the islands of the Pacific, very clearly. Then, on the way from Japan to San Francisco I listen to Manila most of the way, but as we near America I find Quito, Ecuador, comes in better.

Oh, it is wonderful to hear, and that one hour seems so short, for the Christian at sea, cut off from fellowship because few on a ship are interested in spiritual things. But being so cut off from fellowship, one must rely on and turn more to God for fellowship, for the temporal props, which so many lean on, have been torn away and like the Psalmist we can say, "It is no vain thing to wait on the Lord." It is wonderful to be still and to be alone with God, far out on the waters, cut off from the world!

Recently on two occasions I have been in Long Beach. The first time was for a week end and I located the Municipal Auditorium right away on Saturday, looking forward with great expectancy to your service the next day. But how disappointed I was when the ship sailed early Sunday morning. I couldn't see you, but I listened that afternoon as we headed south for the Panama Canal. The last time, we expected to be in Long Beach over the New Year, but were ahead of schedule and left on the last day of the old year. How disappointing! It is highly improbable that I will ever be in California again. I leave America in a few weeks, returning to Britain, and I anticipate leaving the sea. But Brother Fuller, if I do not see you on this earth, I shall meet you in heaven.

The following letter is from Arabia, the land of Mohammed.

Dear Brother Fuller,

For many years when I have been at home, my wife and I were steady listeners to the Old-Fashioned Revival Hour. I am a construction worker and always on the move, and many times I have wished that you could look in on us when your Hour comes on the air. All down the barracks, room after room, no matter how noisy they have been, all quiet down to listen and one could almost hear a pin drop. Your messages in song, and from the Word, have meant a lot to men so far from home. I, for one, am grateful to have been able to hear your program almost everywhere that I have been.

Not only is the Old-Fashioned Revival Hour heard in the land of sand dune and torrid sun, but also under the cold, soft light of the Aurora Borealis. A lady from Alaska writes:

Dear Reverend Fuller,

We are living on a ranch which is forty-five miles from the nearest post office and there are no roads and so no mail service, even in summer. Our only means of ever getting to town is in our small boat. During the winter the frequent storms at sea make it quite difficult to find a safe time to make the trip, so, because of the isolation for long periods, we do look forward to your program with keenest interest, and it comes in so clearly. It is our favorite, as it teaches the plain truth and the way of salvation. It's a comfort to hear you speak often of our Lord's return.

Grateful listeners write from "down under."

Dear Dr. and Mrs. Fuller,

As Dutch migrants in Australia, we want to express to you how thankful we are to God for the Old-Fashioned Revival Hour, and that we can hear it out here in Australia. First in Holland we heard the broadcast from Radio Luxemburg. But when we were out here only a short time, one Saturday night we were tuning to a Sydney station, and suddenly we heard the well-known "Heavenly Sunshine." You can imagine how glad we were, and now we won't have to miss one of your broadcasts. We felt that when we left our homeland we probably never would be able to hear you again. Hearing you away out here is like meeting an old friend.

Here is a good letter from the top of the world.

Dear Mr. Fuller,

Just a few lines to thank you for the gospel messages which come over the air to us here. I am a fisherman, saved by the grace of God over twenty years now! Whether at home or at

19

sea, we listen to your messages, and also the lovely singing. I can assure you it is a lift heavenward, and you do have lots of listeners here in the Shetland Islands. Although thousands of miles apart, it comes over the air just fine. Now, dear Brother Fuller, carry on the good work of gathering in precious souls, and then some day we are going to meet Him, and see the nail prints and the wounded side, and then He will put His lovely hands on your head and say, "Well done, good and faithful servant."

We are praying for you up here.

Before the Bamboo Curtain fell, China's teeming humanity was touched by the sound of the gospel, borne across the vast Pacific on the magic wing of the ether wave. Is it, perhaps, still heard? A missionary, with the China Inland Mission, writes from Kunming, China.

Dear Mr. Fuller,

We have been hearing your program every Sunday evening, and it comes over very clear from Manila. It is a great blessing to us in these Chinese cities to be able to get such a service in English.

Just a few days ago a missionary was here from Tali, who had two Chinese aviators (in the government air force) listening in on your program with them. They were all very much touched by your program and at the close of the message they got down on their knees. One aviator accepted the Lord, while the other was restored to fellowship with Him. So the program is being heard and used of God so far away.

From Bangalore, South India, comes this appeal.

Dear Dr. Fuller,

In His infinite mercy, God has given you the gift of spreading the gospel to numberless listeners through the radio, which reaches from the length and breadth of India. Even though you do not hear from us, still let me assure you that many souls are greatly benefited to hear your spiritual messages of Jesus and His love for us. Thousands who were led astray are eager to turn from their sin to lead better lives. Many have been converted from idol worship to Christianity. A whole town in one of the suburbs of Assam have accepted

Christ and have been baptised through hearing your broadcasts.

These broadcasts of "The Old-Fashioned Revival Hour" by Dr. Charles E. Fuller must be continued and helped by the generosity of the American people whom God has blessed so abundantly. Let not this appeal go in vain. May it turn the compassionate hearts of the Americans to give their help unstintingly to help your broadcasts.

Since the Old-Fashioned Revival Hour is heard in so many places, it not only reaches the multitudes, but also pursues the individual, like a "Hound of Heaven," to use Francis Thompson's startling metaphor. From Minnesota a lady writes:

Dear Mr. Fuller,

I first heard your broadcast in Oakland, California and the Lord began dealing with me then, through your preaching. After moving to a town in Wisconsin, I listened to you there; then two years ago we moved to Minneapolis. It seemed to me as if you were following me everywhere I went and speaking directly to me. Finally, one Sunday afternoon, I just asked God to take over and surrendered my life to Him. About one month later my husband was converted. Truly we have a wonderful Saviour and I know the meaning of forgiveness now.

Dear Mr. Fuller,

Right by my radio, at long last, I have accepted the Lord as my Saviour. I have listened to you for a long time and you have convinced me I am a sinner in need of a Saviour. But I have not wanted to face the facts and I have been very unhappy. I went East to visit my cousins, really to get away from you and the uncomfortable feeling your sermons brought me. But the first Sunday night they turned on your program saying, "We never miss Brother Fuller." The next Sunday I was returning on the train and the porter turned on your program with a broad smile and I noticed several people settle back in their seats as much as to say, "My, how nice. I thought we'd have to miss Brother Fuller."

The international coverage of the Old-Fashioned Revival Hour, though primarily a witness to the peoples of other lands, has incidentally—though significantly—made Mr. Fuller a chaplain-extraordinary to the men of our armed services. One soldier calls the broadcast a "symbol of the things I have been called on by my country to protect." Streams of letters of appreciation from "our boys" and their parents continue to flow into P.O. Box 123, Los Angeles.

Dear Mr. Fuller,

A radio is a lot of excess weight to a soldier when he carries everything strapped on his back, from post to post. Therefore, most soldiers never bother to get a radio, but I got so hungry for your programs recently, that I wrote home and had mine sent to me. I may have a broken back when I get out of the army, but just to be able to listen to your messages from the Word of God will be worth it.

A letter from somewhere in Burma reads:

Dear Brother Fuller,

I never thought the situation that occurred tonight would happen. Some of us soldiers deep in the jungle set up our portable radio and the first voice we heard was yours on your Sunday evening program. We would know that voice and that music anywhere in the

24

world! We heard you praying for the servicemen and your voice in prayer echoed through
the stillness of the night in that dim jungle,
strong and reassuring. Everyone was quiet.
Many bowed their heads in deep meditation
and prayer. And how happy we were, Brother
Fuller, to hear you praying for us servicemen.
As we listened to your sermon we came face to
face with eternity and standing on the brink of
the unknown, some of those men realized for
the first time their need of that wonderful redemption in Christ which I and two or three
others, reared in Christian homes, now know.
We have that redemption, thank God. Out
here so many things that we thought impor-
tant before fade away—the superficiality of
civilized life falls like a veil that covers a sta-
tue, and there stands revealed the truth of the
reason of our existence—and the Cross of
Christ stands high and Caesar's forum crum-
bles. Again, Dr. Fuller, we thank you for the
light that you have cast upon this jungle darkness for us servicemen.

Dear Dr. Fuller,
    Greetings and salutations from your friends
in gay old France. We are on active duty for

the U.S. Army. Last Thursday night my friend and I were sitting parked in his automobile, trying to get some good program on the radio, when all of a sudden, like a memory from the past, I heard the theme song of the Old-Fashioned Revival Hour. I exclaimed, "Listen, that's from California—the Revival Hour, and Dr. Fuller." He replied, 'Oh, I remember him; my family and I listened back home, and it was great!" So we listened. The static was bad for a moment, and a Spanish program interfered, but then it cleared just fine, gained volume, and we enjoyed the whole program immensely. This is the first time since we have been in France that we heard a gospel program. The music and singing, too, were really something out of this world, and it all gave us the extra boost one needs over here, so far from home.

One service man writes: "We Christians in the service enjoy your Hour, but cannot always get it. I was very surprised and pleased to hear you last summer when we were on Attu Island in the Aleutians. The United States Army Special Service Department rebroadcast it for us up there and it was deeply appreciated." In the same vein a young man, now pastoring a church in Kentucky, says:

Dear Brother Fuller,

The first time I ever had occasion to listen to your broadcast was during World War II on the Island of New Guinea. I had just been converted and was very hungry to hear the gospel. Our chaplain was not too much interested but he had some real large transcriptions of your broadcast. His assistant was a buddy of mine and he had access to the chaplain's office. Many nights we would sneak into our grass chapel in New Guinea and play those transcriptions very low, so low in fact that we had to bend our ear very close to hear your sermon. And, Dr. Fuller, you'll never know how dear those transcriptions were to us and several of the young converts way over there in those jungles. Your sermons were easy to understand, and it gave us a good foundation to begin our Christian lives on. I remember very distinctly a sermon entitled, "The Sin Unto Death," which made me see the importance of redemption and of consecrating my life to God.

I am now a pastor of a small church here in the mountains of Kentucky and we get your program at 9:00 P.M. on Sunday night. I recommend to all the people here that they listen, and we try to close our service in time for everyone to get home and hear you. Our peo-

ple are handicapped financially, and I have to
work at odd jobs to help support myself, but
we are in the greatest work on earth, and I feel
that you, Brother Fuller, had a large part in
putting the desire to do this type of work in
my heart. I just want to let you know what a
great blessing you are to me now, as well as
out in New Guinea. It may interest you to
know that one of the fellows who listened to
your broadcast with me out there has now returned to New Guinea as a missionary.

Dear Dr. and Mrs. Fuller,

In Bermuda, where I was stationed as an of-
ficer in the Hurricane Hunter Squadron of the
United States Air Force, it was our wonderful
privilege, while making weather and hurricane reconnaisance flights out over the Atlan-
tic on Sunday mornings, to tune in on the
WB-29 aircraft radio compass, to the Old-
Fashioned Revival Hour. My, how it would
thrill my heart as we rode through the storms,
to listen to the message of the gospel and the
grand old melodies that are so precious to me
as a Christian. Of course, in most cases, I was
the only Christian aboard, and, being the navi-
gator, I was in charge of the broadcast band

selection. So the whole crew had to listen, Christian and otherwise. Several times while flying into the very center of these severe tropical disturbances called hurricanes, as I was twisting the dial of the radio the sweet voices of Mrs. Fuller and the quartet, and, of course, Dr. Fuller and the chorus choir, were heard. It would thrill me to know that, though the wild winds and the storm raged all about me, I was anchored firm in the knowledge that I was kept in peace by the perfect love of Jesus Christ, my Saviour. It was a dangerous assignment, but He carried us through safely.

Not only are Christians in the service of their country, far from hearth and home, encouraged by the broadcast, but many a soldier, straying from the path of right, has, like Hagar in the wilderness, been found of God where he least expected Him.

Dear Brother in Christ,

I returned home from Korea yesterday. It is nice to be back in the States, and nicer yet to be a Christian, which I wasn't when I went away. Now I will tell you a little about myself in the last four years.

When I finished high school back in '49 I

was just a happy-go-lucky kid, and I ran away from home and joined the Navy in September. The first eighteen months I was in medical school and I had to study very hard, but when off duty I spent time with anybody out for a good time. If I could not find a girl for a gay whirl, I spent my time in a bar, which was taking me down to hell fast. But I couldn't see it that way back then. After medical school I was sent over to Korea with 2,500 hospital corpsmen aboard one of our large hospital ships. The fifth day out on the high seas was Sunday, and a buddy and I attended services that night. Our chaplain played a recording of one of your broadcasts, and—oh brother—the sermon sure reached me. That night I was converted. I was in Korea nearly a year, and I had fine Christian fellowship over there.

Now I am out of the Navy and I am in love with a Christian girl, and we plan to be married in September. So I just wanted to write to you, Brother Fuller, and thank you for everything. Keep up the good work for the Lord, and I will be praying for you.

Monica, mother of the great Augustine, followed him with her prayers and had the joy of seeing him come to Christ under the influence of Ambrose's preaching in the city of Milan. A like experience was the portion of the Christian parents who wrote the following letter.

> Dear Dr. Fuller,
>
> We have listened to the Old-Fashioned Revival Hour for years and have been strengthened in our faith and often comforted by your program. But especially do we love it now, for our marine son, stationed out there in California, attended your Sunday service two weeks ago and went to the altar and there accepted Christ as Saviour. We had prayed for him so long, and you can imagine how happy we were to have the answer to our prayers. We were listening alone that day, and though we did not know that our son was there, yet we felt especially impressed by some of the songs. Our son called us by telephone late that night and gave a real earnest testimony and was very happy. How wonderful is radio, that we, out here on the prairies of Dakota, could hear the same service that led our soldier-son to Christ away out there in California!

Besides American G.I.'s, soldiers from other lands have also been reached. A British airman writes:

Dear Brother Fuller,

Just sitting here at some English Christian friend's house this evening having fellowship and listening to the broadcast. I am an airman, stationed at Burtonwood A. F. B., England.

About three weeks ago I was awakened at 1 A.M. in the morning by a man crying by my bunk. He said, "Joe, I want to find God." I got out of my bunk and walked to the chapel with him, which is only about half a mile from our quarters, and there he reeled out a story of his sickness of this old sinful life which he had been living. He told me how he had heard the Word many times and that this night he had come back from drinking beer at the base bar, and was laying in his bunk when your broadcast came on the air. He listened through, and after the message he said he saw clearly his state, and where he stood with God, and he came right over to my hut, crying and "wanting to find God." With the Spirit guiding, I was able to show him how he could find Christ as personal Saviour. He accepted Him that night, and I pray not only as Saviour but as Lord, too.

A young Irish soldier sends the following message from Belfast, addressing Mr. Fuller as his "pastor."

Dear Pastor Fuller,

After professing to be saved before the war, I went into the army, and it was not long till I was worse than the others. In France when things got bad, I prayed to God to keep me safe and I would be a better man, if He would spare my life. I could not do it myself, so I drifted on. It is only God's great love for sinners that I am not in hell for all the things I did. Then this time last year, one night, I put the wireless on and the lovely singing of your Hour came in. It was just great. Then Mr. Fuller spoke on the tabernacle in the wilderness, and he made it so plain how to reach and come close to God and have forgiveness. It was all just wonderful to me, and the next week following, I turned the set on again at 11 o'clock, and again the singing was great. When Mr. Fuller was done speaking, my heart had been so touched, I got out of bed and I knelt down and asked my Lord and Master to forgive my sins, and He did. Now I take all my cares to my Father in heaven and He always hears and answers prayer and helps me. I have never missed one program of yours since that night, and it is just grand to be saved. Thank you for being the means, in God's hands, of restoring me to my Lord. I pray for you and Mrs. Fuller night and morning, and would you do the same for me, that God may use me to win men and women for Himself?

*   *   *

For God so loved the world, that he gave his only begotten Son, that whosoever believeth in him should not perish, but have everlasting life (John 3:16).

People hear the Old-Fashioned Revival Hour not only in *many* places, as the above letters reveal, but also in *strange* places. Letters tell of its being heard in restaurants, drive-ins, and taverns. It is aired on the Super-Chief, deluxe Santa Fe train, patronized by the movie stars, and those who would like to be. An Alaskan fisherman writes he is equipped to receive the broadcast on his salmon trolling boat, since it is the only church the men have on the fishing grounds. Another correspondent observes that of a Sunday he has seen tough water-front men in New York harbor listening to the program and singing "Onward Christian Soldiers" in several dialects. A man in the wool business says, "Many times when the lambing season is on and we are unable to get to church, I have my services and get the Old-Fashioned Revival Hour right here in the sheep barn. I turn it on pretty loud, and the music is fine, echoing above the bleating of the sheep." A lighthouse attendant off the rocky coast of Scotland, who is allowed to leave his post to attend worship only twice a month in the summer, tells of how he looks forward to the Hour (11:00 P.M. on Thursdays). A traveler in Scotland reports that late one night, standing by the sea, he heard sounds, and listening, perceived it was the Old-Fashioned Revival Hour in full swing, coming from the fishing boats returning to port. Speaking of the men at sea, a professional sailor from Vancouver writes:

Dear Dr. Fuller,

I am a master mariner employed on the British Columbia coast. I have a crew of seven on my ship, and I am a Christian and the Lord is really precious to me, also your program. My sailors really enjoy your program, too, for I have it on our loud speaker for them. During the past ten days we have been having a series of southeasterly gales on the coast and often we have to run for shelter. Today we have found shelter and have dropped anchor in a haven of rest; the wind and rain are lashing

35

and visibility is very bad. You sang, "Let the Lower Lights Be Burning" and my, there was power in that song today. Then your message— and you count one more soul, because when you asked for a showing of hands to accept Christ, a young Finnish boy, out here only three months from Finland, understood the way and lifted his hand here on board ship in the storm, wanting to be saved.

Dear Brother Fuller,

I drive a cab in Washington, D.C., and many a happy hour do I spend listening to the Old-Fashioned Revival Hour from the little radio in my taxi. Not being able to go to church much, it fills a great need for me, and how I do rejoice in Christ and all His blessings while I worship with you out there in California. I always ask my passenger if he objects to hearing a fine program as we drive along, and nearly always they say, "Sure, turn it on," but sometimes they seem surprised at what they hear. One flashily dressed lady said, "I haven't heard those songs since I was a child; maybe I ought to go to church again." Some of them make fun, but one man said, "That's what the people of our country need. We'd not be like we are, and in the mess we are in, if we heard and heeded such messages."

If I am driving alone, I sing along with you good and loud; but you can't hear my "amens" away out here, Mr. Fuller. Thank you for coming across to me here in my cab in Washington.

A taxi driver in Britain, who uses the same approach with his customers, writes, "Many [of my passengers] I know have gone straight into their homes to tune in and get the remainder of the broadcast." A lady writes:

Dear Dr. Fuller,

I was visiting my brother in West Philadelphia and we were returning from church on one of those noisy trolley cars, when a young man entered carrying a small radio. My brother whispered rather loudly, "Ballgame." But I whispered back, "No, maybe hymns." The young man smiled and said, "Yes, Charles Fuller's program." I cannot tell you how his face lighted up as he said it, and we knew immediately that he was a Christian.

Another lady writes:

> Dear Rev. Fuller,
> We are on our way to Juneau, Alaska, and never did we enjoy the Old-Fashioned Revival Hour as much as today, Sunday, though we have been listeners for years. But on board ship it seems that nearly everyone drinks liquor, and they seem to think of little else.
> My sister and I share a stateroom with a young lady who celebrated with the crowd last Saturday night, and came to bed about 1:00 A.M. It was terrible in our stateroom by morning. It makes one sick at heart. The celebration went on all night, but they did turn on the Old-Fashioned Revival Hour on the ship radio, and it was wonderful to hear you speak. You mentioned, "Be not drunk with wine, but be filled with the Spirit." From the looks on some faces I think the message struck home —and how good it was to hear the lovely music, too.

The following letter was received from a sailor.

> Dear Brother Fuller,
> Sunday night, after leaving a large church in New York City, we stopped under an awn-

ing, because it was raining. There we turned on our portable radio and listened to the Old-Fashioned Revival Hour. When the rain ceased, some forty people, mostly well-to-do, were standing listening with us. One wished to know more about Christ; one was given instruction in the Word; and one was saved.

Another letter from New York reads:

Dear Rev. Fuller and wife,

Space does not permit me (nor time) to write much, as I must appear with my circus animal act "on stage" within the next hour, but I do want to say how much I have enjoyed your broadcast in the past twelve years or more, and what a comfort they have been to me, for I seldom can go to church.

I am sitting now in my apartment in New York City with three of my employees with me, listening to your wonderful broadcast—tears in two of the boys' eyes, along with my own, as your choir sings those beautiful songs heard so often in my youth. I occupy my apartment in New York only a short time during the year, but I carry a portable radio in my trailer while on the road, and I persuade as many as possible traveling with me to come in and hear your broadcast. On many occasions my trailer is crowded during the full hour!

We have heard you from Montreal, Toronto, and Quebec, clear down to the deep South, and what a blessing it is. We circus people have hearts to be touched as well as anybody, and we need God in the same way that other folks do.

Even a hobo goes to church via the Old-Fashioned Revival Hour.

Dear Mr. Fuller,

I feel I must tell you about an old man that I stopped, with a pack on his back. I asked him if he was a Christian or if he ever went to church. He replied that he was a Christian, but he did not feel like going into church with such ragged, old clothes. "But," he continued, "I have a little crystal radio in my pack, and every Sunday night I stop by some barbed wire fence along the roadside, and I hook my aerial over the fence. Then I tune in on a Los Angeles station, and I listen to a religious program from there. A Mr. Fuller preaches, and I like it fine—both the music and preaching."

So you see, you have a roadside listener who can pick you up wherever he happens to be, and I thought you might like to know of it and offer a prayer for this old man. He may be poor on this earth, but he certainly has a mansion awaiting him in glory.

Dear Dr. Fuller,
Every Sunday morning in our college dorm we could hear the sweet strains of your music floating down the halls from every room that has a radio. If any one dares to use an electric shaver or other static-creating appliance during your program, a number of fellows yell out in protest.

Dear Brother Fuller,
My husband and I live in a box car on the railroad and I cook for a bridge crew. We have to stay pretty close here and keep the fire up in this cold weather, so we do enjoy your program since it is our church. When you all sang "Heavenly Sunshine" and you said, "Shake hands," I walked over and gave my husband a good handshake, 'cause there was no one else

41

around. You would have laughed if you'd seen us.

Dear Dr. Fuller,

I passed a bar in Seattle, Sunday, and it seemed so strange to hear "Heavenly Sunshine" being sung so lustily, and coming out of that place. I stopped to listen for a few moments, and the choir and quartet were singing. Two men were coming out and one turned to the other and said, "My wife listens to that program all the time, and it really ain't bad."

Sometimes not only the wife at home, but the man in the tavern also begins to listen.

Dear Rev. Fuller,

I was in a cafe one night drinking, and your service came on the air and they were going to change the station, but a party was sitting drinking at another table and they said they would like to hear your service through, and so it was left on and we all listened. Now every Sunday night they have your service on in that cafe, and people listen, for they like to hear the music, and they like to hear your message, too, even though they are drinking.

Will you please pray for me as I am a sinner, and I drink and smoke and swear badly, and I want to give it all up. I went on my knees tonight at home alone after your altar call, and I asked God's forgiveness, and I mean by His help to give up these things, and I pray I may be faithful and become a strong Christian.

Not only in a tavern, but even in a house of ill fame someone paused to listen. The propriety of publishing this next letter might well be questioned. Rather than involve the reader in an indelicate disquisition, we solicit the thoughtful reading of the following familiar passage with the hope that it will relieve any possible scruple. "And the scribes and Pharisees brought unto him a woman taken in adultery; and when they had set her in the midst, They say unto him, Master, this woman was taken in adultery, in the very act. Now Moses in the law commanded us, that such should be stoned: but what sayest thou? This they said, tempting him, that they might have to accuse him. But Jesus stooped down, and with his finger wrote on the ground, as though he heard them not. So when they continued asking him, he lifted up himself, and said unto them, He that is without sin among you, let him first cast a stone at her. And again he stooped down, and wrote on the ground. And they which heard it, being convicted by their own conscience, went out one by one, beginning at the eldest, even unto the last: and Jesus was left alone, and the woman standing in the midst. When Jesus had lifted up himself, and saw none but the woman, he said unto her, Woman, where are those thine accusers? Hath no man condemned thee? She said, No man, Lord. And Jesus said unto her, Neither do I condemn thee: go, and sin no more" (John 8:3–11).

Dear Dr. Fuller,

This letter will sound almost sacrilegious to you, but I feel I want to write it. I believe you will understand how I feel. What causes people to go so wrong when they have had a good background? My parents are Christians, my father a minister. I was converted and baptized when I was nine years old. Many times I slipped, but I came back to the Lord. I am now twenty-two years old, and for the past four years I have lived in deepest sin. I was married at eighteen and was blessed with a perfect baby son, who just passed his third birthday last month. It will soon be five years now since I absolutely gave up the Lord. I have tried so many times, but I have no will power, even though I prayed for strength to live a Christian life. I went to a couple of Bible academies and a Christian college, but they seemed to do me little good. To make a long story short, I am now a professional prostitute, working in a house of ill fame. Although I am living a life of sin, I still believe in the Bible and believe in the Lord. It hurts me to hear people blaspheme the Bible and the Lord Jesus Christ.

We have a radio in the house of prostitution where I am now. Your program came on, and I listened. The other girls that work here wanted to turn your program right off, but I asked them to please leave it on. They thought that I was out of my head, but I don't care. It did seem out of place to hear the lovely gospel songs in this place, and to hear you preaching from God's Word. But somehow religious music and the Word of God are never out of place, are they—any place in this world—especially the Old-Fashioned Revival Hour with its message of hope that God loves even the worst sinner! Your program has been known to me for years, but I never had a chance to listen lately, except when I just happened to turn it on today. The next time that I am in Long Beach I shall attend your service on a Sunday.

Please forgive me for writing a letter that seems strange for a girl of my profession, but your program was such a comfort to me today. Even though I hate my work, I can't see any way out of it now. Maybe God will show me a way. I hope I can listen again.

* * *

And he looked up, and saw the rich men casting their gifts into the treasury. And he saw also a certain poor widow casting in thither two mites. And he said, Of a truth I say unto you, that this poor widow hath cast in more than they all (Luke 21:1–3).

Like Müller's orphanage in Bristol, England, the Old-Fashioned Revival Hour is a work of faith, sustained by the free will offerings of God's people, most of whom have their only treasure in heaven. They are rich in this world by faith only; they shall

46

be rich by fruition in the world to come. (A friend of the hour writes from West Virginia: "Dear Brother Fuller, Enclosed is the money from Thursday's eggs. The chickens have certainly started laying since I put them to work for the Lord.")

Dear Brother Fuller,

I am sorry to be a little late with our Christmas offering, but I am glad to have something to send, because the Hour means so much to us. My husband has not had work since November the 1st. Everywhere he goes he is disqualified because he is past fifty, but I am thankful I have a job at the hospital. God knows all about our needs, and He never forsakes us, nor will He!

It is always such a happy time each Sunday when you come to us, and our heartaches and doubts and fears just melt away as you open up the Word of God to us. His comfort flows in. No one preaches like you, Brother Fuller, and we love to hear Mrs. Fuller read the letters, too. We are going to meet you all some time in that "land that is fairer than day."

The poem, "Christmas," in the last "Heart-to-heart Talk" was so beautiful I copied it and sent it to our son who is in prison.

47

A man writes from British Columbia:

Dear Mr. Fuller,

The batteries of my radio set are gone, and now I cannot listen to your words of comfort. God has been so good to me in many ways and I know He will fix things for me so that I am not downhearted until I can hear you again.

I did not have any money to help your broadcast last month, but I traded some hay for a little pig and three dollars, so I am sending part of it and pray that the good work will be carried on, spreading the gospel more and more every day.

Dear Rev. Fuller,

I prayed God to provide some way so that I could have a little part in the Old-Fashioned Revival Hour which I love so much. I knew that we had one crate of berries sold, but how could I get the rest to make up the $2.00 I wanted to send? But today someone came and wanted some berries, so he took four crates. I am sure that if I did not love the Old-Fashioned Revival Hour, I could not have gotten out in the hot sun and worked to pick those berries, but I did. Finally I gave out, so the man helped finish the job. How thankful I am I can have a part in this glorious spreading of the gospel which means so much to us.

Here is a letter from a little girl in Canada:

Dear Mr. Fuller,

I have always appreciated your broadcast over the air. I am only eleven years old and when I listen it just brings me, like magic, to a place of peace. My mother has gone to be with the Lord Jesus about two months ago, and it is very hard for me and my sister, but your broadcast has made us all happy, even my daddy. I was saved about three years ago in a little Sunday school, before I even knew anything about your broadcast. I am sending you ten cents, for I have very little money, but I want it to help you to carry on. Good-by and may the Lord bless you.

Dear Dr. Fuller,

I am a Negro share-crop farmer living in the southeast corner of Alabama. I listen to your broadcast each Sunday and love to hear the truth as you preach it in your gospel.

Some time ago one of our cows on the farm brought us twin calves and died. Shortly one of the calves died. We were successful in persuading one of the other cows to take the remaining calf to nurse and raise. My landlord and I agreed that this remaining calf would be the Lord's.

The Lord blessed the raising of this calf and it has been taken to market and I have requested that half of which I would have shared be sent to you. My landlord is sending equal amount, which would have been his share, to Billy Graham.

We have our regular obligations to churches which we are members of and manage to meet them.

In view of the circumstances we both felt led to do this extra to reach beyond for an extra for our Lord, and chose to call upon you and Dr. Graham to handle these amounts. In Jesus' holy name we ask that you accept this check. Use it, we pray, to reach lost people for the Lord.

(This letter was typed, apparently by the landlord, who may have assisted in its composition.)

Dear Dr. Fuller,

At last we made it. I didn't seem to be able to see my way clear to send any help as the price of hogs etc. is down. And we live on a creek bottom farm where the surface soil is light so our corn crop is kind of a gamble. And last summer the heat burnt the tassels just as they came out. So our corn crop was not too good. But like the song tells us, "God leads the way, traveling through the wilderness." And sometimes we have to wait before we get the marching orders. So enclosed find our offering to help send the gospel out by radio.

And my prayer is that many souls may be saved this year because they heard the gospel preached on the Old-Fashioned Revival Hour, and we could have a little part.

From Kansas there is even more distressing word, but no note of despair.

Dear Brother Fuller,

Just to tell you how sorry I am I could not help out last month. We want to help because the program helps us so much. Perhaps I can explain. May 1st, we had an awful flood that washed out our crops and fences. From the middle of June till August 1st, we had the worst drought I was ever in. The night of August 1st we had a big rain accompanied by severe wind storm and our place was covered with brush. The grasshoppers ruined our corn crop, and this is a lot of disaster for one summer. We will be hard hit for all kinds of feed in this area. I lost ten nice laying hens in two days while our temperature was 112° to 114°. In July we had to buy $250.00 worth of hay for winter. It's hard, but we are thankful for your program and we are still trusting Him.

Dear Rev. Fuller,

I am a 17-year-old boy and I have led a life of sin, and am now on parole from a reform school. Now I am trusting in the Lord to lead me and help me. I used to smoke lots of cigarettes, but by God's grace have been able to quit. I am sending what I would have spent in cigarettes this week to help you, because your program has helped me. I'll be listening to you tomorrow.

❖ ❖ ❖

Come unto me, all ye that labour and are heavy laden, and I will give you rest. Take my yoke upon you, and learn of me; for I am meek and lowly in heart: and ye shall find rest unto your souls. For my yoke is easy, and my burden is light (Matthew 11:28–30).

Though God's people are graciously sustained from despair of the radical kind reflected in some of the letters received, they are not immune to Satan's fiery darts of discouragement as they seek to walk the straight and narrow path up the "Hill Difficulty" to the "Celestial City." Many have written out of their hearts of the *comfort* received through the Old-Fashioned Revival Hour. Thus Mr. Fuller has become not only an evangelist but also a pastor, a shepherd to God's people. Some, like the following, suffer the loneliness of the teeming city.

Dear Mr. Fuller,

I live in the heart of this great city in a shabby little apartment, and I am in my room month after month and year after year with the traffic sweeping noisily by, horns blowing, sirens whining day and night. I am in my late thirties, but I have arthritis and am in bed or a wheel chair most of the time. My husband leaves early for work and all day I am alone, except for my little dog who is very companionable and gay.

Sunday is a lovely day, because my dear husband is at home and together we listen to the program—every word and every note. We can close our eyes and shut out this noisy world outside, and our drab surroundings, and feast on the beauty of God's Word and the heavenly music.

We have so much to be thankful for—knowing our Saviour and having each other. Some people might pity me, but I am happy every day in Christ and leaning on the "everlasting arms" each step of the way.

Dear Mr. Fuller,

I am a city-dweller now because I have a job here, and I tell you that the city is the loneliest place on earth. All week I work hard trying to please our hard-to-please boss, and sometimes by Saturday I am so discouraged and blue and homesick I would rather die than live on.

But I just can't tell you what your Hour has done to me on Sunday nights as I have listened here all alone. The Bible has brought me peace and hope, and I have begun to pray and trust God that my life won't always be this way—so hard and lonely and discouraging. Since I have been hearing your Hour I have found peace with God and He has saved my soul. How thankful I am that your teaching is so plain!

Dear Rev. and Mrs. Fuller,

They call this [Worcester, Mass.] the city of rooming houses, especially down town. Well, we are, by the thousands, in these cheerless rooms; a gas plate, a bed, a bureau, a wardrobe cabinet—nothing homelike; but we do thank God for the radio which brings your broadcast to us. How much it is appreciated, as it lifts us out of these drab surroundings. How I love the hymns, as I used to play the piano for services.

Others write out of the silent solitude of nature's frontiers.

Dear Rev. Fuller,

I am a sheepherder far away from any town away up in the hills. Some people would say that I have a lonely life and sometimes I am very lonesome. Summers I live mostly in a tent, and winters I move into a trailer house on wheels. I have much time to think about God and His handiwork, which I see all around me, and I love the trees and fields and the stars.

On Sunday evening my two companions, who are sheep dogs, and I sit together and listen to your program here in my tent door. Imagine the pipe organ and Rudy's playing coming right here to us! The music is pretty and your sermons mean a lot to me, Brother Fuller. They are like the sermons I heard in the little white church on the hill down in Tennessee when I was a boy. My mother, a saint if there ever was one, always took us children to church, and I was saved in that little meeting house when I was fourteen years old.

Over a year ago I came back from tending the sheep one evening, and turned on my radio. There was your choir singing one of those old songs that I haven't heard for so many years, and I listened through and have been listening ever since, and I tell you, your preaching has brought me mighty close to God and my old mother. I try to hum several of the songs you sing, but I have not heard them for so long, and my old voice cracks, and it doesn't sound so good, I guess. Old Chip looked up kinda funny tonight when I tried to sing, "There is a Fountain Filled with Blood," along with you all.

After you went off the air I sat there in the tent door for a long time, until it got dark, remembering the days gone by. I am sure thankful to God that I had a Christian mother, and I am sorry I haven't lived a better life, but now since I have heard your old-time preaching I have come back into the fold and when my work is done here, I will be going to be with the Good Shepherd.

Dear Rev. Fuller,

I write you this letter for prayer for me. I live alone here in a cabin in the mountains, in sickness and suffering from tuberculosis. I have heard your radio programs so many times, but here a short time ago my radio tubes grew weak, and I was so depressed not to hear you until some good neighbors had the radio mended. How I enjoy and drink in every minute of the Hour, but the seconds slip by so fast and then it is over for another week, and I am so sad. I get very lonely. I may not be here when you come on the air next week, but if not, I'll be in heaven, free from all pain and loneliness, because I heard of my Saviour's love over the Old-Fashioned Revival Hour, and I accepted Him.

From Scotland a lady writes:

Dear Sir,

I am sure when you read this letter you will understand why I wrote to you last Thursday. I tuned as usual to your broadcast on Luxemburg and it met a great need of my heart. My husband, who has been off work since October 11th with cardiac thrombosis, had had one of his very bad days. My little girl was fevered and tossing with tonsillitis. My oldest boy, aged nineteen, had written to tell me that he was coming home on embarkation leave and would then leave for Malaya. My coal bill was unpaid and I was told I was to get no more for heat until it was paid, and the cold here is bitter. I was very tired and weary, from lack of sleep—my heart was heavy, in fact, my load seemed almost too heavy to carry. Then, as I said, I tuned in to your Revival Hour as I always do. You introduced your son, Dan, to us, and I could not but hear the love and pride in your voice. Dan's prayer warmed my heart a great deal. Then you all sang:

> I need Thee, Oh, I need thee;
> Every hour I need Thee!

And when it came to the chorus I, in my trouble, sang it with you, though my voice shook. Then the floodgates opened and oh, the blessed relief of those tears. After a while, God spoke and I felt better and began to take heart and to think things out like this: my blessings; I still had my husband with me, thanks to God; my little girl would, God willing, be better tomorrow; I would at least have my son at home for 21 days, and if it was God's will he would be as safe in Malaya as elsewhere. I decided to ask the coal firm to accept a weekly payment and clear my bill, and perhaps I could manage to buy my little girl a new pair of boots by the time she was ready to go back to school. Things suddenly seemed much brighter, and I didn't feel so weighed down with worry. Now, Mr. Fuller, I'm quite convinced that when things seemed so dark that night, God Himself had said, "Cheer up, take heart, things could be much worse." And I did. Therefore I will always remember that night when God met my need and I shall hold you in real affection and gratitude, and if things are difficult at times, as they will be with my husband unable to work, it will help me to know that you and your son, together with "Honey" and others, are praying for me.

Dear Mr. Fuller,

In a few hours the ambulance is coming to take me home in Salisbury, where a flag-draped casket is waiting with the remains of my only son, just returned from Europe, and where we will lay his dear body away.

I felt that I could not bear it, for my heart was broken, but I turned on your program which seemed to be prepared just for me. Your choir sang "Does Jesus Care?" and then "Take your Burden to the Lord," and then "Wonderful," and then you gave such a precious message from God's Book. How it thrilled my soul when you sang,

> On that happy golden shore,
> Where the faithful part no more;
> When the storms of life are o'er,
>   Meet me there.

My burden is lighter because I realize more fully that I am not going down to that service today alone, for God will be with me, to strengthen me.

My son was a pilot, and he said in one of his last letters, "I never feel alone when I am up there. When I ask God to help me, I feel a surge of calm courage." Mr. Fuller, that is what I received from your service this morning—a surge of calm courage. Thank you for the comfort your broadcast brought into my sick room at this time of great need and the consciousness it brought that God is with me, and He cares.

Many, in the midst of poverty's corroding cares, have, through the Old-Fashioned Revival Hour, found the words of our Lord fulfilled: ". . . Go and shew John again those things which ye do hear and see: The blind receive their sight, and the lame walk, the lepers are cleansed, and the deaf hear, the dead are raised up, and *the poor have the gospel preached to them*" (Matthew 11:4, 5).

Dear Rev. Fuller,
     We are just poor folks, trying to raise enough on our little farm to feed the family,

and to get the place paid for. We work hard, but never seem to get ahead, likely because the soil is poor and we are so far out in the country and have to haul so far. We don't have much to do with, and it is lonesome, and would be discouraging if we did not know the Lord.

Two years ago our oldest son worked for a farmer near town, and bought us a good radio. He is away in the service of his country now, and my, what that radio means to us no one will ever know! Sometimes the tears run down my face when we turn it on, and the beautiful, heavenly music of your choir comes right into our little house—just like it goes into the finest city homes—and to our boys in the camps and hospitals, and so many other places. It sounds like heavenly music, and the pipe organ, too. I have never been in a fine church, with a big organ, but I don't have to, because we have the finest organ music in the country right here in our little home on Sundays.

And, Mr. Fuller, when you preach, you make God so real to us, and the Bible so plain.

Dear Friend in Christ,

I have wanted to write to you for some time to tell you of the great blessing your program has been to our home of eight. Three years ago I started listening to your program. We have an old battery radio because we have no electric lights in the house. We live up on a hill in the middle of the woods, but thank God, when the Holy Spirit speaks to hearts it don't matter where you live or what you live in, or how poor you are. I sat by the radio many times that first year while you gave the altar call and I thought, does God mean forgiveness for me, too? I knew I was spiritually lost, but it didn't seem possible that His gift of eternal life and forgiveness could be for a person like me. Then one Sunday when everyone had gone fishing for the day, I listened alone and I fell on my knees and cried out to God for His mercy and forgiveness, and praise the Lord, He entered in, and later in our little country chapel I acknowledged my Lord as Saviour. Oh, the change in my heart and life and home since Jesus came into my heart! I started praying for my unsaved family and God is answering prayer, I am sure, for they have all led godless lives and it is going to take time, as it is the Holy Spirit's work that convicts us. I try hard to live a loving Christian life before them and I know that helps, but oh, the years I wasted not living for the Lord.

Every Sunday morning the first program we

turn on now is the Old-Fashioned Revival Hour, and what a way to start our Sabbath Day! The music sure is so refreshing and it speaks to hearts. We can't send any money offering because we are so poor, but I thank God that I can get on my knees and help pray when the altar call comes on, and all during the week, too. I thank God that He has some real old-fashioned preachers who preach the message of salvation. Some people would like messages to suit this modern world, but praise the Lord, He is the same yesterday, today, and forever. Jesus never fails. That verse led me to see that Jesus does not fail if we repent and believe and live for Him. I am not a good writer, nor well learned in English, but whatever we have we can use for God's glory, and that is what I am trying to do.

Dear Brother Fuller,

My wife and daughter were looking for some fresh eggs out on a back country road one day recently, and they came to a very dilapidated little building all falling to pieces and out in front was a sign, "Fresh eggs are for sale." My wife went to the door and knocked and a very poorly clad, but clean lady came to the door. My wife said to her, "Oh, you have Brother Fuller's program coming on your radio." The lady's face lighted up and she said, "Oh, it's just wonderful for us. We never can go to church, but he brings the most beautiful music and sermons true to the Word of God right here into our little home."

Out of her heart, a woman writes with touching pathos:

Dear Brother Fuller,

Thirteen years ago I lived out in the woods in Mississippi. We were so very poor, and we had no radio, of course. Our neighbors had a battery set and every Sunday we would gather around that radio with them, and oh, how you have comforted my poor heart many times when there was no other way to hear about Jesus and His love! It always touched my heart when you would say, "Go ahead, Honey," for I never had anybody to be kind to me. But today I have Jesus, and He is all I need. I love you, Brother Fuller, your wonderful group of singers; and may you have many, many years to help poor souls like me who have no love and kindness in their lives until they know of God's great love which is everything. We had no way to go to church; you were all we had. God bless you forever.

A moving letter from Nebraska reads:

Dear Brother Fuller,

You are our comfort-minister. Of all the good gospel ministers we hear on Sunday, you, above all of them, truly comfort us with your message of cheer and understanding. I have gotten up on Sunday morning, sometimes with a heart so heavy, so full of dread and fear and loneliness, that I cannot explain to anyone how the load was lifted when I turned on the radio and heard "We have heard the joyful sound, Jesus saves!" One Sunday Mrs. Fuller said that she believed that her husband was the most beloved man in the world, and I believe it, too. We know you have had trials and testings, Mr. Fuller, and so you can comfort your great radio audience, all who are going through deep waters. I have never failed to gain strength and courage from your messages.

My husband and I have suffered the loss of

everything. Once we were independent farmers. We didn't own a farm, but we had stock and all the necessary equipment, but today my husband is a farm hand. We live fifteen miles from our town. We have no conveniences except lights. This winter we lived in our kitchen and kept warm by burning cobs, because we did not have money to buy coal; but oh, Mr. Fuller, God is so wonderful! I could drop to my knees and thank Him for those cobs, and they did not cost us anything. God never forsakes us. My husband and I marked all the promises from the tract you sent us in our Bibles and we are standing on those promises, and reminding God daily of them. And, oh, praise His name, I now rest in Him because I know He is going to save my dear, wayward Johnny, who is spending three years in a reformatory. Our lives have been sad, and our hearts have been broken, but did anybody ever suffer like our Saviour suffered! I know the trial of the road will seem nothing when I come to the end of the way.

And so, dear Brother Fuller, the precious truths we've learned from our heavenly Father, through you, are worth more to us than all the wealth of the whole world. The theme of your whole hour of broadcasting, the singing and all, is comfort. And oh, how we need it in these trying days when the pressure is so great. Thank you with all my heart for your testimony—for making Christ so beautiful, so real, so precious, so desirable! We can never come to see you, but we will meet you up in heaven, and we are going to sit down together and "tell the story how we overcame."

Not only the saints in general, but ministers in particular, like Samson of old, have their fainting fits. Paul writes in a remarkable autobiographical passage: "We are troubled on every side, yet not distressed; we are perplexed, but not in despair; Persecuted, but not forsaken; cast down, but not destroyed" (II Corinthians 4:8–9). Mr. and Mrs. Fuller find it most heartening when word comes in of some servant of the Lord who has through the ministry of the Broadcast, renewed the oil in his lamp. The following is typical.

Dear Dr. Fuller,

I am a Presbyterian missionary in Utah, and have for years preached the gospel to cowboys, loggers, and people in isolated places. We hold services in homes, ranches, cook shacks, wherever we can, and your program has always been a great blessing to me and an encouragement.

Especially do I remember one Sunday when the going was hard and I had to travel 150 miles to get to my preaching appointment. The road seemed long and weary as we traveled over the mountain passes, and through miles of sagebrush. I tuned in on the Old-Fashioned Revival Hour as I chugged along in the dust and I heard the hymn, "I'll Go Where You Want Me to Go, Dear Lord," being sung so beautifully. It just fit the need in my soul that morning, it encouraged me as I hummed along with you. So you see, brother, you preached to a preacher, and I sang with your choir. God bless you, brother!

The rural areas of our land have many closed churches. Denominational leaders are so concerned about the tendency of young men to use the country church to get to the city church, that special courses have been offered in some theological institutions to encourage young men to spend their lives in the rural parish. In view of these considerations, letters like the following from New York State, signed by

James, John, Peter, Beth, and Allen, are most significant.

Dear Brother Fuller,

For twenty-one years of ministry in rural churches, your broadcast has been a harbor to our souls. In storm and tempest we have found safe mooring. In disobedience we have received rebuke and then fresh orders; in sorrow, comfort; in despair, courage; out of confusion, clarity. This and much more than we can ever tell has been imparted to us through your faithful ministry of the Word. We thank God for you and uphold you before the Throne of Grace. May this anniversary be the beginning of the best year yet.

The following letter from missionaries in the heart of darkest Africa was given Mrs. Fuller by a friend. It reads:

Dear Brother and Sister in Christ,

The one thing that we have purchased recently which wasn't absolutely necessary and yet which we felt very definitely the Lord had

led us to, was a radio. Since we are so cut off
from the world and we never knew how the
war was going from one month to the next, we
have wished for a radio. But we never had the
opportunity to get one. Then accidentally (if
things are accidental with God's children) we
happened on to a radio with a new battery
when we were in search of a battery for our
truck. We had searched in vain for one and it
meant our truck would not be in running order until we got one. When we found this new
battery, we were overjoyed to find the man
would not sell the battery without the radio.
The Lord had so unexpectedly sent us there
that we felt after prayer and consideration that
we should take both—especially since we had
no idea of when we would find another battery. So the one battery serves for the truck
and radio too and the truck charges it for use
in the radio. The radio is a used one, but it is
in very good condition with all new tubes. We
hear the war news from England and the
U.S. every day. Also heard Charles Fuller's
Old-Fashioned Revival Hour Sunday night,
even though we did have to stay up until 11:00
p.m. to hear it. What a blessing it was to our
souls to hear good old-fashioned gospel singing after these four long years! It was like a
nice cold drink to one dying of thirst in a des-

ert land. Then we heard a wonderful message by Rev. Fuller and our hearts were thrilled beyond words.

From England a happy minister writes:

Dear Mr. Fuller,

Quite recently it was my joy and privilege as an elder, a minister of the Christian Church, to interview a Mrs. Lewis in Liverpool, who had made application for baptism and membership, during the course of which I listened to a most amazing story of conversion. Some two years ago now Mrs. Lewis and her husband were listening to the radio one evening and had not found anything really interesting or impressive until, quite by accident, the little baby daughter who was sitting on her mother's knee suddenly twisted the dial and they got the Luxemburg station. "Oh, it's a religious service," they said. "Let us leave it on for a few minutes and see what it's like." It was a Thursday and the Old-Fashioned Revival Hour comes through clearly here in Liverpool. Gradually they both became interested in the wonderful singing of the hymns that they had heard years ago, and then your sermon really gripped them. Each of them felt that God was really speaking to them, and when you asked those who desired to accept Christ as Saviour to raise their hands, Mrs. Lewis, being under deep conviction, was constrained to do so, sitting by her radio. She then went to her knees and surrendered her life to God. Meanwhile her husband had retired to bed, and she quickly followed to tell him what had taken place, and to her great joy she found him on his knees by his bedside; he also had yielded his life to God. This was two years ago, since which they have gone on in the love of the Lord, and say they never knew what real joy was until and since that day Christ came into their lives.

As one who listens whenever I can on Thursday evening, I do feel the urge to pass this on for your encouragement. You are doing a wonderful work and there must be thousands in this great city of Liverpool who enjoy every moment of your services. Although we have never seen you, we feel we really know you and love you and remember you continually in our prayers. If you ever do come over to our country (we hope that you will some day), we should rejoice to meet you in our church here in Liverpool.

A young clergyman ministering to a church rich in tradition, and in whose ranks have served some of the greatest divines of all time, writes:

Dear Dr. Fuller,

It may be a surprise to you to have a letter from an Anglican priest in Britain, but I feel that I must communicate with you to express my sincere thanks for the "breath of fresh air" flowing across Europe from Radio Luxemburg on Thursday evenings. I feel that the Old-Fashioned Revival Hour has caught something which has probably been lacking in our churches too long. My only regret is that by the time your address reaches us it is usually twenty minutes to twelve, midnight. Recently when my father came to visit us (he, too, is an Anglican minister), we both stayed up late to listen to your program and thoroughly enjoyed it!

As I am only in my third year in the ministry of Christ, I feel that I still have a lot to learn which the years at college did not touch upon. I should be most grateful if I could have some of your addresses in printed form. Of course, your style of preaching is rather different from that heard in the pulpits of the Church of England, yet, perhaps, by your help this may be to some extent remedied in one pulpit at least.

What this young Anglican clergyman had in mind seems to have been realized by a layman in Montreal, Canada, who writes:

My dear Dr. Fuller,

A few years ago I turned on the radio in my home one Sunday morning and through a Vermont station came across your service. The old hymns which I had never heard in my own high Episcopal church, took me back to my days as a boy, when I heard them at my Sunday school in England. I gave my heart to God that day in my study, and asked His guidance. I wrote you and received a wonderful letter in return. Since then what changes have occurred. All my life I had ridiculed the doctrine of salvation, my life was wrapped up in ritual and sacramental teaching.

When my rector asked me to start a Bible class in his ritualistic church, I accepted the invitation. We began with 24 people and ended on May 2 this year with 960 persons every Sunday afternoon. I have 30 denominations in my class. We use your hymns and your techniques, and are beginning this fall with a crowd of 1200. The past year has seen over 600 souls brought to Christ.

Gone are the days when bridge was a mania with us; gone is the liquor which was always in my house. Gone, too, are the friends who desired the material things of life. I did not have to give these worldly things up, they gave me up!

Starting Sept. 30 I shall be sending you a regular tithe for your work. On April 1, I gave up half my business to operate a problem clinic in my church. My rector is a transformed man today. He, too, knows the living Christ. I preached in a cathedral in May and shocked the staid persons there by asking everyone to shake hands as you do. This caused great consternation in such a place, but we now do this in every church; I want happiness and friendship, I want to show what the love of God within us can do to humanity.

I am so grateful for your work; your message brought the answer to the prayers of my mother and sister, who always had regretted my type of religion. I have been privileged to bring my message to a dead church which is now in process of revival in this, the second largest French speaking city in the world.

Like Paul, Mr. Fuller may say, "I have planted, Apollos watered; but God gave the increase" (I Corinthians 3:6). A couple of home missionaries from Idaho write:

Dear Dr. Fuller,

Going about from house to house in this rural community, as we speak to people about their soul's salvation so many tell us that they accepted Christ as Saviour just by their radios. In other cases people's hearts have been prepared by listening and we have been able to lead them to Christ. Oh, the need for personal work is very great. We always recommend people to listen to the Old-Fashioned Revival Hour unless they do so already.

This letter is from a young Presbyterian minister.

Dear Brother Fuller,

For ten years I have enjoyed the Old-Fashioned Revival Hour. But I have often wondered, is it really doing its job, is it reaching the unsaved? It is fine that the Christian is strengthened as he listens, but do the lost tune into this program? I will confess that I did not think so.

In pastoral calling on the unsaved in this, my first charge, I was amazed that everybody knew of the "Heavenly Sunshine" man. Many listen regularly. Best of all, they listen not only to the fine music, but just as eagerly to the message as well. "It is the best music on the radio," I am told, "and Reverend Fuller speaks so simply that even I can understand." And these are unsaved, unchurched people of whom I am speaking. The Holy Spirit, through your broadcast, has planted the Good Seed and now I am privileged to come along and reap the harvest.

Last month I was enabled to lead to the Lord a coal miner who was in the hospital after being severely crushed under a rock slide. Every rib, as well as his back, was broken. While under the rock he had cried out, "God help me. If I die now, I die in my sins." Now this man had been a real prodigal. He had wasted his substance in riotous living. He knew that he was a sinner and needed salvation, but where had he learned this? After I had talked with him, and he was gloriously converted, I learned that he had, in his unsaved state, listened to the Old-Fashioned Revival Hour and you had made it plain to him that he was a sinner in need of a Saviour.

Thank God for the heart preparation that bore fruit in this mighty work of salvation.

* * *

Then Jonah prayed unto the Lord his God out of the fish's belly, And said, I cried by reason of mine affliction unto the Lord, and he heard me; out of the belly of hell cried I, and thou heardest my voice. For thou hadst cast me into the deep, in the midst of the seas; and the floods compassed me about: all thy billows and thy waves passed over me (Jonah 2:1–3).

Wherefore he is able to save them to the uttermost that come unto God by him, seeing he ever liveth to make intercession for them (Hebrews 7:25).

Every sinner, apart from God, has lucid moments when he knows that all is not well with his soul. In a few individuals this sense of anxiety is heightened, by circumstances, to desperation and a determination to end it all. The voice of Mr. Fuller has been the means, under God, of plucking some of these brands from the burning.

Dear Brother Fuller,

I certainly appreciate your broadcast, for I do not believe I would be here to face the new year, if I had not heard it under unusual circumstances. I had drifted away, and was far from God and backslidden and in deep trouble, and one day on returning home from work I found a letter addressed to me saying my wife had left and taken the babies with her, and that she was not going to return. I read the letter, and I was so shocked that I was really frantic. I dearly loved my wife, although I knew I had been far from kind and considerate of her.

I drove speedily to her father's home to talk and beg her to come back, but I returned home without her or the babies. I was so grief-stricken and I did not care to go on living without my family. That evening I decided I could not stand it and planned to end it all. I closed the garage up tight and started the car motor going, and turned on the radio to listen and make the going easier. I lay down near the exhaust from the car, and in a short time I felt my head thumping and felt myself slowly going out of this life, but I did not care. Nothing seemed to matter, as far as I was concerned, and the quicker I went the better.

The radio was going and it sounded like a

loud racket. My head roared and boomed like a jungle drum. I hoped all would soon be over. Then I heard a powerful voice speak on the radio. Everything was dark and I do not remember much. Then I heard this voice speak again and it was speaking to God in prayer. Then I began to think of God and the hereafter and I realized where I was going if I went out now, for my sinful past seemed to press upon me.

I don't know how, but I crawled like a helpless creature to the door and pushed it open. The fresh air helped my awfully aching head and I just lay there and listened to most of Brother Fuller's sermon, and I knew I wasn't ready to go, and I felt a terrible fear in facing the future. I pulled farther and farther out into the air, but I could still hear. I shudder when I think of how near I came to eternity. I didn't talk to God even then, but He surely was watching over me. I couldn't eat, I couldn't sleep, for I knew I had to choose between God and Satan. I thought I couldn't bear my cross and I wanted to get away from it all.

I am now at home with my father and mother, and they have been so kind. This new year found me at church, praying to God as I have never prayed before, for His forgiveness and for the restoration of my family. It hasn't come yet, but I know that God is all powerful, and I will do my part, and am asking Him to do His. How thankful I am that your program was on the air, and that it came just in the nick of time or I would have spent an eternity in hell!

Dear Rev. Fuller,

Several years ago I was in a desperate state and on the way out to the barn to commit suicide. The whole family was away that Sunday afternoon—dark and cloudy—and my spirit was as dark and hopeless as could be, for a most bitter disappointment had come into my life, and I wasn't living close to God, so I did not have the comfort of prayer and trust in Him.

As I went out through the dining room I flicked on the radio, I guess to put off a few minutes what I had made up my mind to do, but was dreading to do. I heard your quartet singing. It sounded so good and I sat down for a minute. Then you began to preach, and it was right to me that you spoke. You said, "Jesus said, 'Come unto me.'" I sure was heavy laden and I came and He gave me the rest He promised and things have turned out for the best.

When I look back, I know that God answers prayer and when we turn our lives over to Him, things work out right, no matter how hopeless they may seem.

Dear Mr. Fuller,

My husband hauls wood, and a strange thing happened as he delivered a load to a blind man who lives all alone. The man's house was so neat and well kept and he was so cheery and smiling, and even if he was blind, he was able to count out the money perfectly to pay my husband. After they chatted awhile and my husband was leaving, he asked the man if he ever heard Charles Fuller preaching, and he told him that he would like the *music* on that program, too. The blind man smiled broader than ever and said, "Say, mister, I never miss hearing that man every week. Several years ago I had cataracts on my eyes and the doctor thought that he could cure them, but he wasn't able to and the nerves in my eyes were killed and I've been blind ever since. I was awful discouraged, living alone since my wife died, and I was desperate and felt there was nothing ahead for me. As I sat in my sitting room I was half-way listening to the radio and I got up and went to the bathroom shelf where I have some sleeping pills and I was going to take enough to kill myself. I was so blue. But while I was hunting around the program changed and the music caught my attention and I went in and sat down and listened to the rest of it and to Mr. Fuller's sermon. Well, you know, it cheered me up so, and I never did find those sleeping pills, but I found the Lord as my Saviour soon after that, as I continued to listen. And do you know, I've never been alone or lonely since then. When I get to heaven, I'm going to shake Mr. Fuller's hand and tell him he not only saved me from taking my life, but he introduced me to my Saviour. And what's more, I can see Brother Fuller then, and see how good looking he is."

Dear Rev. Fuller,

Several years ago I was a young violinist who showed great possibilities of a brilliant future, according to my instructors. Due to an unavoidable accident my hands were badly broken and smashed. Although the doctors did all they could, my fingers became stiffened and crooked. The disappointment was so keen, and I felt so hopeless, that I stayed in my room constantly, not even attending church. I became very bitter, and sorely abused those who wanted to help me. The years passed and I became more and more convinced that this world had no place for me.

One very dark day the horrible idea of destroying myself came into my mind and I was convinced that was the only way out of my suffering. My mother begged me to attend church with her that Sunday morning, but I refused, as usual. While alone in the house, I placed on the table the box of sleeping pills and made my plans to go out the easy way.

As I sat there, writing a farewell note to my folks, I became dimly aware of a radio next door, the song coming through open windows. I found myself leaning out the window, almost against my will, listening to your voice coming from the radio. As the beautiful singing continued, and your words of prayer reached my ears, it seemed as though you were speaking to God and I felt His presence so very real. It seemed that a chunk of ice around my heart was slowly melting. Then as your pianist and organist played "Leaning on the Everlasting Arms," I dropped to my knees and as the whole group sang "What a Friend We Have in Jesus," I began to pray. The wonderful meaning of the words of that song sank in deep.

I am so glad I heard you that day. Dr. Fuller, and that God spoke to me through you. May I tell you in closing that I am happy now, as I opened a small book shop in a nearby city, and my whole outlook on living has changed. I know that I am a child of God, and am living a normal, happy life, thanks to His redeeming grace.

My dear Dr. Fuller,

Last Sunday night as I was walking along the streets of this city [St. Louis, Mo.], a cold wet night, no place to go to sleep or no bed to lie down on, a heartsick and discouraged man, I walked into the YMCA to get out of the rain. As I sat there, sure enough, your broadcast was turned on and I sat and listened. I was so discouraged. I had in my pocket three tablets of poison ready to take. But I heard those old songs and the one that hit me the hardest was "Bringing in the Sheaves." Right after that you said a word that somebody may be listening that is thinking of taking his life. Well, I was that one. I listened through the broadcast to your message, which touched my heart, and afterward I went to the washroom and threw the tablets away. Then I went outside to a small park that is close by. By then it had stopped raining and I got down on my knees and gave my heart to God on that wet ground, in that little park.

Well, if no other good came out of that broadcast, it did do good for one man, and that is me. And may God bless you in your work for Him. I know God as my friend now, and I am sure He will open up the way for me.

*　*　*

Praise ye the Lord. Praise God in his sanctuary: praise him in the firmament of his power. Praise him for his mighty acts: praise him according to his excellent greatness. Praise him with the sound of the trumpets: praise him with the psaltery and harp. Praise him with the timbrel and dance: praise him with stringed instruments and organs. Praise him upon the loud cymbals: praise him upon the high sounding cymbals. Let every thing that hath breath praise the Lord. Praise ye the Lord (Psalm 150).

Thousands of letters have been received expressing heart-felt thanks for the ministry of music on the Old-Fashioned Revival Hour. As one man from England comments, "The musicians amplify the message of the song." The unusual merit of this phase of the program is due to the fact that all the musicians happily combine professional training and devotion to Christ. They are not only born musicians but born-again musicians. They not only know how to sing, but they believe what they are singing. God has given them their songs. The music is planned and directed by Mr. Leland Green, coordinator of music in the Pasadena Public School System, an early convert and devoted friend of Mr. and Mrs. Fuller.

Dear Dr. Fuller,

I have been an interested listener to your radio programs for some time. What first caught my attention was your singing my mother's old hymns that she used to rock us kids to sleep with, i.e. "Throw Out the Lifeline," "When the Roll Is Called Up Yonder," and "I Need Thee Every Hour." I am a pretty tough old hombre, and I have knocked around this tough, old, indifferent world for seventy-six years—thirty of them in the show business. Consequently, I have quite a tough hide, quite a crust, but you get me in a corner when I listen to you preaching and singing those old songs that my dear old mother used to sing to us, which I had not heard for many, many years, by reason of being in the show business so long. You may preach to a man until you are black in the face, but when you get him to singing those old gospel hymns that his mother rocked him to sleep with—well, you touch his heart.

An amusing letter from a child in Michigan reads:

Dear Mr. Fuller,

I just want you to know that I listen to you every Sunday and enjoy your program very much. I think that Rudy plays better than Liberace! I am eleven years old.

The reviews of some of the music critics are even more enthusiastic in their praise.

Dear Rev. Fuller,

I have two babies and cannot always go to church, but the Hour is my church when I have to be at home, and how I do love it! I hope the Old-Fashioned Revival Hour quartet and chorus will be the official quartet and chorus in heaven, and that Rudy will be the official pianist. (One correspondent writes, "I have a little canary that's ten months old and is just crazy over the choir and quartet and especially Rudy's piano. He'll only sing his best when the Old-Fashioned Revival Hour is on. . . .")

* * *

And behold, a woman in the city, which was a sinner, when she knew that Jesus sat at meat in the Pharisee's house, brought an alabaster box of ointment, And stood at his feet behind him weeping, and began to wash his feet with tears, and did wipe them with the hairs of her head, and kissed his feet, and anointed them with the ointment. . . . And he said unto her, Thy sins are forgiven. And they that sat at meat with him began to say within themselves, Who is this that forgiveth sins also? And he said to the woman, Thy faith hath saved thee; go in peace (Luke 7:37, 38; 48–50).

Though it is a blessed truth that God gives His people songs in the night, there are those who have no song—only the night. We will not encumber the following letter with commentary, but simply remind the reader that our Lord was a friend of publicans and sinners and a close friend of Mary Magdalene out of whom He cast seven demons.

Dear Mr. Fuller,

Sitting here in my shabby room located in this city's real skid row, I tuned in my squeaky worn-out radio and heard the singing of those old sacred songs. Oh, how I used to love them, and how I used to love to go to church! When I think of those days in the far past, it doesn't seem possible that that carefree, happy girl could be the same person sitting here in this dingy room, and I *am not* the same person I was twenty years ago. Then I was innocently ignorant of the pitfalls and ways of the world. Today I am a wretched, wrecked soul, drifting with the tide, one of the unfortunates who are so despised, a hopeless drunk, I am called, but I know what I am. I am one of the hundreds of alcoholics here in this city. Some were strong enough to find sobriety and a normal life through Alcoholics Anonymous, but I am one of the many who have not been able to grasp it. My mind never seems to get clear enough for me to think straight. I am helpless,

Mr. Fuller, and I have long since decided that I have no choice but to continue to drift with the tide and become a complete derelict.

I have been trying to keep myself clean and to keep my hair from becoming straggly so people won't point to me and say, "Look at that drunken hag!" Ah, Mr. Fuller, if people who are not afflicted as I am, would only try to understand and be a little tolerant, how much better chance one would have to obtain sobriety and right. No one knows what might come in their life. I never tasted an alcoholic beverage until I was twenty-five years old, and I knew I was an alcoholic from that first drink twenty years ago. I gave up, or I might say, lost a fine position as head buyer in a large department store, in a large city far, far from this city. I realized there was something so wrong with me, because I could not leave drink alone and I could not bring disgrace on my family who were, and are, if they are still living, the essence of honor and respectability. Of course, they think I am dead long, long ago. Here in this miserable existence I still work, cleaning or anything honorable. Right now I am washing dishes and cleaning the kitchen in a greasy lunch joint here in skid row. I can't work very good if I drink too much, so I keep taking sleeping pills while working. That is worse than being a "wino" as we are called. I have to save every nickel to buy pills and wine. So many times I decide that it is no use any more, and many times I have tried to end it all by the "goof-ball" route. But something happens every time and I don't die.

This morning I was thinking of it when you were saying about someone might be discouraged, and then I decided to write to you, but I don't know why, because there is no hope for me, an alcoholic and "goof-ball" addict. Sometime I will end it, maybe any day. I don't believe God will help me. I believe in Him, though, and it is my fault if He don't, but I would die by inches if I should give up drinking. It is just too late now to do anything about it, and I must just drift on with the other lost souls as long as I can get liquor. After that I don't think, and after writing this letter I am not going to think of the days before I became a slave to this stuff. Neither am I going to turn on my radio again on Sunday. I do not ever want to get your program or any other one that will cause me to realize that I was once somebody and respected. No, I must keep on telling myself that I have always been just as I am now, and any other thoughts are an illusion or only the result of too much wine or pills, hallucinations in other words.

93

I do not know why I am writing to you. I borrowed the paper and envelope and pen from another derelict just like me, for we are all of a kind in this dump. This is the first letter I have tried to write for ten or twelve years. I have almost forgotten how to write. I used to be well educated. I am sending a dollar, but I do not know what for, but I think I am using it as an excuse for writing. I can't spare it, but will eat less or nothing for the next week—but I must have my drink.

In my wretched, miserable life I am proud of one thing, that even though a hopeless drunk I am a good woman morally. No one would believe it if I told them that here, but I am proud to know it myself. I am not asking you to pray for me, it is no use, but I feel better now that I have written this letter than I have for a long, long time, so long that I can't remember. Your voice is very kind, Rev. Fuller, and I know you preach the truth, for I do believe in God. And your music is so beautiful that words could hardly express how lovely it is.

Since this letter contained no signature or address, all efforts to throw out a lifeline were stymied.

The letter was read over the air and the wealthy Christian lady volunteered to give every assistance in building the life of this woman anew in Christ. This information was likewise broadcast, but the offer—if ever heard—could not induce the poor soul to reveal her sad secret. Finally, after many months a second letter was received.

Dear Rev. Fuller,

I have not listened to your program since I wrote you several months ago, until today. But I am sorry I ever heard your program here in this shabby skid row. I had adjusted myself to this miserable life, but now I am all mixed up since hearing your music and hearing you preach.

Oh, Mr. Fuller, I do want to stop drinking and be normal, but I can't stop. No one would understand. Today you sang two of my favorite songs that I used to sing in the choir so long ago, "In the Garden" and one about, " . . . though vile as he, takes all my sins away." Once I believed that, but I forgot all about it as the years passed—the awful years—and I was contented when I was half-drunk. But since hearing you, I do not find contentment in the bottle; but I am tormented day and night, utterly hopeless. What *can* I do?

When I started this letter, I fully intended to ask you and Mrs. Fuller to pray for me, but I know that isn't the answer; there is no use, for I can't help myself. Sure, I believe in God, but He can't help me, because I am so weak and I cannot help myself. If I could only die! I have tried, but now I haven't the courage to take my miserable life. How can a person come to this depth, Mr. Fuller, a person who is well educated, capable of holding a fine position, once highly respected? Since hearing your program I am not satisfied but in the pit of despair and remorsefulness. I cannot do any different though.

Again there was no signature and no address. The liquor industry may atone for the above sin with bigger and better television programs to help us all laugh and forget, but the following letters, characteristic of many received at the Old-Fashioned Revival Hour office, are a far happier antidote.

Dear Brother Fuller,

Another year is coming to a close and with it come memories, many memories of the past. This New Year week also is the eighth anniversary when God saved me and healed me from alcoholism in San Francisco's Skid Row. I fail in words when I give thanks to God through Christ for these wonderful Christian years. I also thank God that He has a faithful servant like you, Brother Fuller, for it was those simple words over the radio that went into my heart and changed my whole life, i.e. that whatsoever you ask of God in Christ's name it shall be given to you. I asked Him with all my faith for cure from the alcoholic drink and He heard me and my despairing cry, for I had been an alcoholic for thirteen years, one of those that medical science cures till their best friend and weakest moment catch up with them. But when God takes the desire away, it's gone forever. Only a drunkard really knows what I'm talking about. I promised God in exchange for His healing me from the condition, I promised Him the price of a show ticket whenever His collection plate goes by, and that's how little I knew about Christianity. I did know the Salvation Army collected money, even in saloons and beer dives, wherever they are permitted to enter, so that's where my promise idea came from. But I have learned better now, and my prayers for your work will always be that you may reach the down-and-outers, as I was, to give them new life even after the best years have been wasted as mine were. God bless and keep you and give you strength to spread the gospel to this sinful world.

From Britain a letter comes, signed "A broken-hearted lieutenant colonel."

Dear Sky Pilot,

Tonight I am making a confession I dared never make before. I am and have been a hard-living, hard man. I have fought in most of the major battles of the last war and have several decorations and campaign medals for gallant and distinguished service in the field. After many years of war, I came home to a family that did not know me or want me and my children did not know me or want me. I have tried to live with them, but I am a stranger, an interloper in their midst. The wounds received in the war and from my family, have driven me to drink. I have lost my personality, my character, and my desire for life and what it means. I have drunk and drunk for hours to try to forget. I am despised by my wife and by my daughter, after giving them everything in life. Can you imagine what this means to me? The little income I have left I spend entertaining friends I meet in bars and hotels. I call them friends, even if I meet them just for the evening. At least I have company; I am not alone.

Tonight I am staying at a little hotel in the Great North Road near Bow Bridge in Yorkshire on my endless travels. I have been drinking, trying to forget for a few hours. At a quarter to twelve tonight, March 17th, I came into my hotel bedroom the worse for drink. When I went down, I had left my wireless switched on and your program was on the air when I came in. The organ was playing and your choir was singing; it was beautiful. You asked people to kneel and pray and ask God to take them as they are and forgive them, and you said that He would, no matter how scarlet the sins might be. Maybe you won't believe it, but the service touched me deeply. I knelt and prayed and did as you asked, and this is my confession. I could not help it; I just had to do it. Maybe I was a sentimental fool to do this, and to write this letter to you. Do you know what it is to be lonely, unspeakably lonely, wandering the countryside, no home, no friends, frittering your meager finances away? There is only one end to it all, but if anyone ever needed your prayers, I do! Thanks for a few minutes of peace and happiness. I'll listen again.

This next letter is a most remarkable one in every way. The statement on the perplexing problem of the relation between man's will and God's power would do justice to a theologian.

Dear Fuller Family,

Our God, who is so wonderful to us all, has saved my soul. I was such a terrible drunkard, but saved by the grace of God. I know I found God just in time, or I would have died in my sins. I couldn't even hold a bean-picking job at the last. In fact, I couldn't hold anything. I've drunk hair tonic, rubbing alcohol, vanilla extract. I sank lower than a snake, but the love of God lifted me up. That was two years ago, the 26th day of last November. I was in jail before that eighteen times for being drunk in that year; ten months all together. Some say it is will power. Well, it sure was; it's my will, but it's all God's power, because I never had any!! I am now fifty years old, but I feel twenty years younger than I did ten years ago, so you can see what God has done for me. Now I want to make up a little to our heavenly Father for giving His only begotten son to save the world. When He saved me—well, He will save anybody!

*   *   *

And, behold, there was a man in Jerusalem, whose name was Simeon; and the same man was just and devout, waiting for the consolation of Israel: and the Holy Ghost was upon him. And it was revealed unto him by the Holy Ghost, that he should not see death, before he had seen the Lord's Christ. And he came by the Spirit into the temple: and when the parents brought in the child Jesus, to do for him after the custom of the law, Then took he him up in his arms, and blessed God, and said, Lord, now lettest thou thy servant depart in peace, according to thy word: For mine eyes have seen thy salvation (Luke 2:25–30).

With the increase of our life expectancy through the advance of medical science, and the perfecting of liberal pension plans, living in retirement is becoming a *bona fide* branch of sociological science.

Yet it is still true, for the most part, that the cares of the aged are a concern to no one. What better consolation than that of the gospel can be given these lonely inhabitants of the land called forgottenness? Let him who doubts peruse the following letters.

Dear Brother Fuller,

I have lived over time—past 80—and my hard-earned savings are just about gone, but your services are my greatest comfort. I am here alone in my apartment and very crippled. I keep saying "the Lord is my shepherd, I shall not want." I wish I could help with the broadcast, but I cannot. Please keep sending me the "Heart-to-Heart Talks" which I let my friends read, and they are a comfort to us all. We do need your prayers, Brother Fuller, all we lonely, old sick folks.

Dear Rev. Fuller,

I live in this old folk's home, in bed all the time, 83 years old. How I do love and look forward all week to your service each Sunday. I used to sing in the church choir, when I was young and pretty, and they said I had a good voice, too. The wonderful man I married said he fell in love with me when he saw me there, singing in our little white church choir, on a bright May morning. I remember I wore a bunch of lilacs on my shoulder that day and we were married in that little church the next year. My memories are very sweet. Many years have passed since then, and here I am, a wrinkled old lady, just waiting for God to call me home to be reunited with the loved ones, and to look on His face. I feel His presence is with me all the time, and when the Old-Fashioned Revival Hour is on, it almost seems that I have gone to heaven, the music is so sweet. The program just feeds our souls and encourages us old folks to keep on.

Dear Rev. Fuller,

I am a lonely man living on my farm, and I just want you to know that since my wonderful Christian wife died nearly two years ago, I have hardly missed a Sunday hearing your broadcast. I sat here alone every Sunday night last winter with our yellow cat, Buttercup. He is old, too, and likes the warm fire. Mother and I used to listen together, but her chair across the table is empty now and my heart and life are empty too, since she is gone. She used to pray for me, for she was a wonderful, sunny Christian, but I was stubborn and never would give up and accept the Lord and come out and out for Him, even if I have always really believed. About two months ago, one Sunday night while you were preaching, I just made up my mind I was an old fool and I got down on my old knees by Ma's chair and I just asked God to save an old sinner for Christ's sake and He did. I wanted you to know about it. Ma may be a little surprised when I get to heaven, but I don't believe she will be, for she believed that God answered prayers and she sure prayed for me a good many years. I wish I had come before she went. She would have been so happy.

One radio friend from Oklahoma wrote of a devoted couple each about seventy years old, who walked a mile and a half every Sunday night to her home to hear the broadcast. The husband had to make the round trip with the aid of two canes, but as they listened, their faces would light up as with the light of heaven. Their son finally purchased them a radio. Another aged couple, also helped by the program, write as follows:

104

Dear Dr. Fuller,

My husband and I are too old and broke down to walk to church and we have no other way to get there. Our health is gone; nothing coming in. We listen to your broadcast every Sunday and must say that it surely helps us to trudge on in the long, lonely journey. It makes us know that God does love us, even when we are old and broke down, and there is a home in heaven for us, where we won't be old and lonesome any more.

Those who care for the aged are sometimes blessed in their being blessed, and so the gospel's comfort is compounded.

Dear Dr. Fuller,

I surely do praise the Lord that He enables you to carry on the Old-Fashioned Revival Hour. I have invalid parents; Mother has been an arthritic cripple for ten years, and Dad has been blind and in bed for over two years from a broken hip. February 7th, this year, he raised his poor frail hand at your invitation, Dr. Fuller, and murmured, "God be merciful to me, a sinner." How delighted I am over this, as he is 87 years old. He is still a babe in Christ, but he prays to the Lord, "Help me to do everything that will be pleasing in your sight, oh, God," and oh, that prayer is mine, too, even though I have been on the glory road about twenty-five years.

Dear Mr. Fuller,

I wish you could look into this Old People's Home as you send out your program Sunday nights. I am a nurse here and I thank God there is this one glowing spot in the week for these dear old people to talk over for seven days and to look forward to. We have early supper Sunday night and they are waiting, some of them being in their places in the library for half an hour before time. Some have napped just before time so their mental faculties will be at their best. Fourteen old folks sit in a circle, and to see their faces shine when your first song comes on is a real inspiration. As the program goes on, many a withered cheek is wet with tears as the old songs bring back memories and the faltering voices sing with you on some of the old songs. They sing "Heavenly Sunshine" with you and, oh, they are so disappointed when it is not included in the program. They all love your sermons and one dear old man, a Methodist minister, to whom heaven is so real and so precious, always says when you finish, "That boy's preaching the truth, he's got it straight, God bless him. I pray for him. You all carry on in prayer for him when my chair here is empty. I'll be up there waiting when that boy comes, and I want to shake Charles Fuller's hand when he gets to glory, and hear the Saviour tell him he was true to the Word."

* * *

For I am not ashamed of the gospel of Christ: for it is the power of God unto salvation to every one that believeth; to the Jew first, and also to the Greek (Romans 1:16).

The power of the gospel testified to in the above letters has been mysteriously felt, even by those who are strangers to the grace of God, as one may discern in the following correspondence from Great Britain.

Dear Dr. Fuller,

I just chanced to turn on the Luxemburg station and heard your broadcast at eleven o'clock at night. I write to you with admiration and respect, not as a Christian believing in Jesus Christ. You may think it is impossible for an unbeliever to take inspiration from either your religious hymns or your sermons, but indeed that is so in my case. I have hesitated over writing this letter, fearing it may seem to be an insult. Yet I may achieve something by showing that a skeptic is not necessarily a scorner, that a non-Christian does not have to feel hostile toward Christianity.

Your Revival Hour services contain a mystical element which reaches me as something entirely new, fresh and strong. You've been preaching on the Epistle to the Romans, a letter written centuries and centuries ago; also, a part of the Bible very familiar to me through readings by my headmaster in evening prayers at boarding school nearly twenty years ago. St. Paul wrote them; my elderly headmaster read them; but you presented the ancient message in such a way as to compel attention.

Dear Dr. Fuller,

Your name and broadcast have become household words over here in Scotland, not only among Christians, but among the unsaved as well. I work deep in the mines where Christians are outnumbered easily one hundred to one. But even in the bowels of the earth, among ungodly men, I have heard your broadcast being discussed many, many times. You may rest assured you are doing a good work, bringing the gospel and the facts of eternity before men and women the world around and in places where a Christian worker cannot enter, thus reaching the unchurched.

Evidently even some Communists have a hard time choosing between Karl Marx and Jesus Christ. From a village in Wales, where laboring men must stay up late to hear the Old-Fashioned Revival Hour, comes the following letter.

Dear Brother Fuller,

We want to thank you for your broadcast from Luxemburg. We do enjoy the services just wonderfully. If you could see, or rather imagine you could see, our valley here at this late hour of the night, you would see hundreds

—yes there must be that many, of people who tune into your service. And what is most amazing of all is that in this mining village we have many Communists who listen to your broadcast. They have told me so, and they enjoy it, too. May they learn the truth from hearing you. One Communist had his set out of order, and he rushed to another person's house to listen in to your service. This person was a Christian and was glad to have him there.

Tell your singers that they sing beautifully. Welsh people know good music when they hear it. (One correspondent writes from a little mining village in South Wales, "You come on at eleven o'clock at night, and you can tell in this village that people are listening by the lights in their windows, and your messages bring that Greater Light—the Divine Light of Him who said, "I am the Light of the world."

Not only Communists and skeptics, but also Roman Catholics enjoy the Old-Fashioned Revival Hour and sense the power in the truth of the gospel. We observed above that the broadcast is widely heard in the Emerald Isle. But there is evidence that our Catholic friends are helped not only in the land of the shamrock, but also here in the United

States. They write from various parts of the country. One greeted Mr. Fuller as "Dear *Father* Fuller." Let us hear what some of them have to say.

Dear Brother Fuller,

Remember me? I told you I was a Catholic, but I hope it won't make any difference between our friendship for, as I told you before, I just live for Sunday nights to come to listen to your wonderful broadcasts. You just get next to my heart, and it seems like you almost make us better Christians right away. I hope it is not a sin for us to listen, for your preaching does lead people out of darkness, and to want to live for God.

This unusual letter from the East Coast was written by a young boy.

Dear Mr. and Mrs. Fuller,

I am twelve years old. I go to St. Mary's school. I am in the eighth grade. I have three brothers that are bishops. They all graduated from a theological seminary and they just came home from the army. I am a great listener of your radio programs. I have one sister who is a nun.

Now the thing that I would like to say in my letter to you is this. My mother won't let me listen to your radio programs any more. She says that we are not of your faith. She says that we are Catholics and should not listen to others than our own.

But I told her, "Mother, they sing so beautiful. It won't hurt me any." I told her what a wonderful talker you were. But she forbids me to hear your programs any more in the house. So I said to myself, I have a little radio that I can carry around with me. So this Sunday night I will be waiting to hear you on the air at 7:00 o'clock. I wish you were not so far away, because I would be there every Sunday night. You know I play the piano and sing in the choir of our church, so if you all will sing for me, "Let the lower lights be burning, send a gleam across the way," I will be listening for you all in my attic.

Thanking you all ever so much.

Dear Reverend Fuller,

I've been listening to you for over a year now, and you've helped me to make many decisions. I was brought up a Catholic and I was never happy. Many things made me wonder. But a year ago last February I stopped fighting God's call and became a born-again believer in Christ.

Last September, the day I was to be baptized as a Protestant, I had some fear and some doubts, but I listened to your program that day and you spoke words that gave me grace and strength to trust and obey Christ. The Lord has been wonderful to us. Both my husband and I love Him very much. Our oldest son, nine years, asked Jesus to come into his heart; where, had we remained Catholic, it would have been so much different. Now our lives have changed greatly; where once we quarreled, now we love and are happier than in years. But every happy sky has a dark cloud, so some day God will put a silver lining in that too, for some day my Catholic parents will say that I may come home again.

I want to thank you from the bottom of my heart for the sermon you had on Easter Sunday, on the Second Coming. It touched the bottom of my heart and filled my soul to overflowing, and I can't explain it, but I felt God's grace as I have never felt it before. I had never heard, until yesterday, that Christ would return to this earth, and I wish I could have a copy of that sermon. God bless you always, Brother Fuller.

* * *

When the even was come, they brought into him many that were possessed with devils: and he cast out the spirits with his word, and healed all that were sick: That it might be fulfilled which was spoken by Esaias the prophet, saying, Himself took our infirmities, and bare out our sicknesses (Matthew 8:16, 17).

Jesus enjoined His disciples to minister to the sick and endowed the early church with the gift of healing. Less directly, perhaps, than St. Francis or Florence Nightingale, but no less truly, the Revival Hour Broadcast has brought comfort and healing of mind to many disconsolate, languishing on beds of illness. Because of the vastness of his audience, conservatively estimated in the millions, every Sunday someone hears the gospel from Mr. Fuller's lips for the first time and someone for the last time. Richard Baxter, the Puritan divine, once remarked that he always preached as "a dying man to dying men" and the voice of Mr. Fuller carries a like earnestness, a sense of which, on the part of his hearers, is reflected in the following letters.

Dear Rev. Fuller,

An old man, a carpenter, had been brought down from the mountains very sick. At the hospital the nurse turned on the radio to get the Old-Fashioned Revival Hour. But as he was so sick she thought it best to ask him first if he cared to have her leave the program on. So she asked him and he said, "Oh, yes, please leave it on to the very end. I want to hear it all." He listened intently all the way through, and just after the service ended he passed away. God only knows what that message may have meant to that dying man.

Dear Mr. Fuller,

I am working as orderly at a charity hospital here, and am writing you from the ward. Your program has just been turned on and probably before you go off the air, some in this ward will pass on into eternity; others, maybe, before another program next Sunday. But we thank God that these people are hearing the Word of God plainly given, and many of them are prepared to meet God and are saved by the precious blood of Christ because they have been able to listen. We do thank God for your program that brings messages of consolation to men who are passing on to eternity. As I look in the ward from the desk here, the nurses and some patients are gathered around the radio. I have just closed the eyes of one man who, while your choir was singing "Think of the Home Over There," passed on to meet Christ, and his last words were, "Tell Brother Fuller I will meet him over there." Oh, how these sick people are hungry for the gospel! I am an ordained minister working here as an orderly, and I thank God that I can turn on your program each Sunday and that it brings peace to the dying, consolation to the living and salvation to the sinner.

Dear Rev. Fuller,

I am a twenty-four-year-old boy and I have a pretty bad sickness with tuberculosis. I have been in bed for over a year and do not know that I will ever be up again. The fight seems to be a little too much for me.

I have listened to you all last winter and up to now, and I never could tell you the good your whole Hour has done me. Christ is real to me now, for I have accepted Him as my Saviour here in the dark, alone. After one of your broadcasts last February, just after you went off the air, I began to pray to God and He accepted me as His child and forgave my sins.

Prayer means so much to me now and I can truly say that even if I am bedridden, my days are happy. My mother died when I was a baby and they tell me she always prayed that I might be a Christian. The Old-Fashioned Revival Hour has answered my mother's prayers, and it may not be long until I meet her in heaven.

Another young man, almost the same age and afflicted with the same dread disease, has this radiant testimony.

My dear Mr. Fuller,

I am a young man, 23 years old, a sufferer from tuberculosis and I have been in bed for the most of three years now. I never can find words to tell you what your Hour has meant to me in the last year that I have listened. My whole outlook on life has been changed and I can truly say that I now have peace *with* God in my heart and also the peace *of* God. This terrible sickness came on me rather suddenly when I was in college, and the first thing I knew I had a hemorrhage from the lungs and the doctor said I'd better leave Pittsburgh and come out here. So Mother and I came, with me on a stretcher, and here I've been in this little screened room nearly ever since. Oh, how rebellious I was to have all my hopes knocked in the head, and I used to curse my fate and say that if there was a God, I hated Him. One day I heard your music and I liked it, and then I began reading my Bible and I could hardly wait for the next Sunday to come. I can truly say now that I love God and His Word, and I've won two souls for Christ: our milkman and an old man who comes to cut the wood and do chores for us. I'm getting weaker, Brother Fuller, physically, but stronger in the inner man, and if it isn't God's will to heal my body, I'll be glad to go home to heaven any time He calls me. Oh, Mr. Fuller, if only everyone could know the joy of the Lord and what He has done for one poor sick boy! Radio is such a wonderful thing to reach the shut-ins.

After five and a half years in an iron lung, a man from Binghamton, New York, who had no use of arms or legs, learned to operate a sensitive touch electric typewriter with a stick in his mouth. With his new-found skill he typed a very neat letter telling of blessing received from the broadcast. From quite a different part of the world, one afflicted with the same disease wrote as follows:

Dear Brother Fuller,

After being a shut-in for the past six and a half years and a prisoner of the iron lung because of polio, I had come to feel that there was nothing left for me in this old world. After being afflicted by that terrible disease, I was left paralyzed from my chin to my toes. But I have come to know that my physical loss has not been in vain, for by my illness I have found the Lord Jesus and learned of His love for me. He has given me something to live for, for which I am greatly thankful. So I am writing to tell you that out here in Honolulu we look forward to the time when we can hear the Old-Fashioned Revival Hour, which we all love so much. If it were not for this hour, I am sure that this gospel would not have reached many of the remote spots of the earth that it has reached, and because of it, many like myself have heard of the Saviour and their lives are made bearable.

119

From Albuquerque, New Mexico, a brave girl writes:

Dear Dr. and Mrs. Fuller,

I have waited all day anxiously in this hospital room to hear the Old-Fashioned Revival Hour and finally at four o'clock it comes in so clearly and heavenly to me. I shall be depending on you for the two or three months that I shall have to be in this hospital. You don't realize how much a message from God's Word and heavenly music can quiet one when in the deepest sorrow. My heart was torn in pieces a week ago, and all things changed for me in the twinkling of an eye; but then, only three weeks ago, I was the happiest girl on earth. Yes, I was the bride of a most consecrated young man, who was planning to serve the Lord as a Baptist minister after being discharged from the Navy. We felt that we had a long time to serve God together, as he was 23 and I am 21 years old. But only a week ago my husband was taken from me in the worst accident the Albuquerque police had ever seen. I was underneath the complete wreckage of our car, and they thought I was dead. Only a miracle could save me, everyone thought, and I know the Lord did save me for some reason, though I don't see it now. I have tried to think that maybe through this accident we were able to witness more in a few days than we could have in a whole lifetime.

Since I have been in this military hospital, I have tried to witness in my sorrow to those about me. I have heard so many remark how wonderful it is to see a Bible on the night stand, instead of a package of cigarettes. Then I've heard others say they have never seen anyone take such deep sorrow with more faith and courage. They would also add, "The secret is in that Bible she has on her stand." At least, they know that I have the Lord with me.

Dr. Fuller, I know you have so many requests for prayer from all over the world, but I hope you will pray for me that I may be used for God all the remainder of my life. I am far away from home in another state, so it gets pretty lonesome, but how blessed is the Old-Fashioned Revival Hour to bring me peace and ease the pain. My husband and I were driving west, hoping to see you when we reach California, but maybe I will have that privilege of seeing you some day. I have not ever heard such beautiful music as you have on your program. Your quartet sang, "No, Never Alone" today, and oh how those words sank into my weary heart!

In closing I just want to say with all my heart, God bless you, Dr. Fuller.

* * *

And [he] brought them out, and said, Sirs, what must I do to be saved? And they said, Believe on the Lord Jesus Christ, and thou shalt be saved, and thy house. And they spake unto him the word of the Lord, and to all that were in his house. And he took them the same hour of the night, and washed their stripes; and was baptized, he and all his, straightway (Acts 16:30–33).

The family is the basic unit of society. The breakdown of the home in our day, reflected in the rising divorce rate and increase of juvenile delinquency, has alarmed all right-thinking people. What is the answer, if it be not the gospel? In the New Testament we read of whole households converted to Jesus Christ and baptized into the church, and there are many Christian families in our land today because of the Old-Fashioned Revival Hour. In others God has begun the good work, converting some who, like decoys, are seeking to lead their loved ones into the gospel net.

Dear Mr. Fuller,

I wonder how many can remember what you preached many years ago. It was between 1923 and 1933 that we used to pile our entire family in our Ford and travel to Placentia to hear you. You probably had not been preaching long, for you were still referring to "orange grove days." It was a small church there. Afterwards, when you first went on the radio we sat in on some of your broadcasts given upstairs over a shoe store in Long Beach. We have listened through the years and prayed for you and your broadcast and have sent offerings from time to time along the way. When the children were home, during the years at Westminster, your program was on, I suppose, without a single lapse. Our son, John, who will graduate from seminary this June, wrote us that he had been listening to you back there in New Jersey. "It reminded me of our Sunday afternoons at home, Mother," he wrote. Our daughter, when a missionary in China, before the Communists caused them to leave, wrote,

"Whom do you suppose we heard over the radio today?—Mr. Fuller! It surely made us happy." And we have a big forest ranger son in the North, who enjoys listening to you, also. Yes, Mr. Fuller, you have had a great part in teaching our children, and have been a great blessing to us through the long years. My, how we have enjoyed the wonderful music of the quartet and chorus choir! In closing I want to say that my husband and I thank God for the Old-Fashioned Revival Hour.

Dear Rev. Fuller,

Your program has come into our home for many years, and what a blessing it has brought us! An incident occurred when I was eleven years of age which I would like to relate to you. One Sunday afternoon the Hour was on the air and the quartet was filling our home with music. I came downstairs to listen and, to my astonishment, I found the house empty. I sat down alone when suddenly my Dad stood up from behind the bookcase where he had been for some reason, and he said, "Weren't you afraid that the Lord had come and taken us all away?" "Oh, no," I answered, "I knew the

Lord hadn't come because Rev. Fuller was still preaching over the air."

Dear Reverend Fuller,

I listen with a very sincere prayer that you may continue on the air with your wonderful Hour. Life would be such a blank for so many of us without the Old-Fashioned Revival Hour. But I sometimes think your beautiful music is somewhat wasted on us, as we all join in singing with you, and almost drown out the choir; Grandma, in her squeaky voice, Mamma in her high voice that gets everyone else off, Dad in his uncertain bass, Edith, aged six, with her little girl squeak, and Joy, aged three, can't sing well as she needs her tonsils out, so she sorta croaks, and our little neighbor of six, Pat, who sings quite well, and her little brother who can't sing at all, but enjoys trying, nevertheless! Anyway, we all love the Lord and want to sing His praises.

I must also mention that your messages from God's Word bring joy to our hearts. It is the message this poor, tortured world needs so much. Yes, you bring moments of sunshine into the lives of all of us and we pray that you may continue on the air.

Dear Reverend and Mrs. Fuller,

This letter is long overdue in thanking you for the excellent program, both music and messages, which has helped mould my life for almost eighteen years. When I was small, our family was unable to attend Sunday services in the city during snowy winters. Instead, we would gather around the radio and listen attentively to the Old-Fashioned Revival Hour. And how we loved it! Then one night as you were giving the invitation, I stood up from my usual place on the floor in front of the radio, squeezed my little six-year-old eyes tightly shut, and asked the Lord Jesus to come in and cleanse my heart. And He did. How clearly that experience stands out in my mind, as well as the time when the Holy Spirit again used your broadcast to bring me closer to Himself, when I was twelve years old.

Today, about to depart to New Guinea as a missionary, I am eternally indebted to the godly training in our home and to the ministry of your radio broadcast. I know that any fruit which we shall see over there will be a direct result of our having heard the Old-Fashioned Revival Hour as we were growing up. God bless you as you continue to work for Him. We hope we will be able to hear your program in New Guinea in the future.

Dear Doctor Fuller,

I have often thought to write to you folks and let you know you had a big part in my salvation. Thanks be to God for His goodness, and forgiveness. You see, in 1948 I was living in Billings, Montana. It was a life of living hell for me in those days, as both my husband and myself were drunkards and Saturday would find us both in the beer halls in the afternoon while our three dear children sat in the car outside. We would generally go home at 5:30 P.M. and have supper and then go off to all the night clubs, leaving the little ones in the hands of a baby sitter. We would arrive home in the early hours of the morning, arguing with each other, and many and many a time those arguments would turn into real fights. How my heart would ache for a real friend. You see, all my people lived in Australia and I felt so alone.

I had remembered a letter that my dear sister had written to me as I left Australia, telling me of

"What a friend we have in Jesus,
All our sins and griefs to bear."

One of these drunken Saturday nights we had a big fight and Sunday morning found us both

sick and sorry. I switched on the radio and sat
and listened to dear Dr. Fuller. It seemed as
though the message was just for me, and when
the appeal came I knelt by my radio and asked
forgiveness for all my sins. I told my husband
that I would quit drinking, and he told me it
was O.K. with him, but he wasn't going to
quit. I loved my husband dearly and told him
I would do just what he wanted me to do. If he
wanted me to drink with him I would, so for
many weeks after, I was under great conviction
and Sunday mornings always found me waiting at 8 o'clock to hear your program. God
knew my heart and He sent two of His dear
saints to our front door. They came back and
offered to drive us to church, and one Sunday
I decided to go, and I really found Christ as
Saviour. I felt so different and I felt I could
not, nor did I wish to go on living in a sinful
way, and I was determined by God's help to
quit drinking for good. I told my husband of
my decision. The pastor came to see us the following Tuesday and invited my husband to go
to church. He did and, praise God, he was
saved too.

Oh, but only God knows the change that
came into our hearts and lives! The desire for
all drink and cigarettes and worldly pleasures
left. Our home is such a wonderfully happy

place now since Christ took over. We have our family altar each night, each one praying from the youngest one up, and we just delight in hearing your broadcast every Saturday night at nine o'clock here in Australia.

I might add that many ungodly people out here just love to listen to the broadcast. I pray that they, too, might come under conviction, just as I did. Oh, if I could only tell the world the love, the peace, and the joy that they would find in Christ, and to awake out of their sin, shame and misery, before it is too late. I know, because I have experienced both lives.

Dear Brother Fuller,

As you can probably tell from the address, we two girls, with other nine brothers and sisters, parents and aged great-aunt, live in the slum area of Chicago. We always stay up late, especially in the summer when it is so hot that our three-room upstairs apartment is like an oven. We had our twenty-year-old radio on the other night, when we heard your program. That was the first of June and since then us two sisters have been listening ever since. Our brothers, sisters, parents and great-aunt listen once in a while. Our mother at first didn't approve for us to listen, but father didn't mind, so we listened anyway.

Your program has been a source of constant inspiration to us, and we hope you will do as we are doing and pray for the conversion of our brothers and sisters. Jim, 21 years old, works at a hotel, and since my father is lazy and drunk most of the time, Jim supports us. George is 19, but he takes after Dad. Ruth is 18; she is going to have a baby, but is not married yet. Ann is 16; she is still in high school and real pretty and popular. Mary and I are next; we are twins, in the 10th grade at high school. Next are Bill, 13, Elizabeth, 10, Jane is 7, Joyce and Bob are twins, they are 5, then there is Mom and Dad and great-aunt Matilda. Please pray for them, too. We all need to know God. [A minister in Chicago searched for this family but was unable to locate them at the address given.]

Dear Brother Fuller,

We have just listened to the Old-Fashioned Revival Hour and we think it is the most wonderful work on the air. We are just a young couple, married only three months ago. At that time we were both in sin. We liked dancing and lots of other pleasures of this world and we bought us a radio two weeks ago and accidentally ran across your program and the very first time we heard it we repented of our sins. We wouldn't miss one of your programs for anything. We hate the things we once loved. Now we have our family prayer every night. We are as happy as any couple could be, because you have brought us to Christ. We hope your programs continue on the air and we're sending you a contribution of one dollar hoping it will help you to continue your good work.

Dear Mr. Fuller,

Just a few lines to tell you that hearing you in the last few weeks has brought a hopeless sinner to Christ. I left my wife eight months ago and came to California, but I listened to your program and your messages reached my wicked heart. I have found Christ and the meaning of love, and I am leaving shortly to meet my wife again and my two children. I am out of work, but starting life all over as a Christian husband and father.

Dear Mr. Fuller,

Words can't express to you the joy in my heart since my dear husband has been converted by listening to your services. Such a change you never saw in your life. Oh, the times he has cursed me for having your program on when he came into the room, and he has made me turn it off when I wanted to hear you so bad I could have cried. But I have kept on praying for his soul that God would work in his hard heart and make him so unhappy he couldn't stand it the way things were. Well, he took sick and I don't know whether God did it or not, but he wasn't seriously sick, but he suffered a good deal, and I was just as patient as I could be in taking care of him, and it wasn't very easy because he was so cross; but I prayed and was just as kind and gentle as I could be. Then Sunday came and it was a pretty long day for him lying there in bed, and just before you came on I asked him to listen to your beautiful music and he did and liked it, and when you began to preach he listened through, and the next Sunday he asked me to turn on your program over an hour before it was time. I set it to the station, but didn't turn it on, and then ten minutes before time he had me turn it on so he wouldn't miss it. He was just as quiet as could be through the whole service, and then when you gave the invitation, Mr. Fuller, he said with tears in his eyes, "Betty, I am an old sinner, but do you think God can save me? I'd like to be saved and cleaned up and live a different life, and treat you different for you are a wonderful wife." Well, to make a long story short, he was gloriously saved and changed and he's reading his Bible now and going to church as soon as he is able to, and I am so happy I am ready to burst. Praise the Lord; He surely does answer prayer.

Dear Mr. Fuller,

My husband and I listen to your program regular and it is changing us. We are both in our teens and last summer we were in every scandal and were the talk of the town. And we haven't settled down yet. We know we are on the wrong path, but all we know is people like ourselves who smoke, drink, and run around and everything.

After we hear your program, we want to do different, and then we are still at it. It took a lot of courage to write this letter to you, 'cause it's the first time we ever broke down, but after we heard you preach some sermons we wish we could change. You say that even the lowest, most damnable sinner can be saved. I believe we are way beyond that, so if your prayers can help, let's have them. It is worth a try, even if we lose.

My husband has never been inside a church in his life, and since I got married I haven't either. If prayer can help us, it will be a miracle. God bless you and keep you on the air so we can hear you, and we'll be listening.

Dear Rev. Fuller,

One day, some years ago, in our home in the State of Washington, my husband and I were listening to your broadcast. We were both perfectly miserable. I had my head in my hands, crying softly, for I did not want him to hear me. We were both chain cigarette smokers and I was a heavy drinker, really a drunkard. He was lying on a cot while we listened to your program and suddenly, as you were still speaking, he lifted his hands high toward heaven and cried from the depths of his heart, "Oh, God, save my soul." I jumped up and ran over to him and knelt down by the cot, and we both asked God to forgive us. We accepted Christ as Saviour as best we knew how.

I did not even know that the precious Bible

said, "Old things would pass away, all would become new," but that very thing happened to us. That night as I laid my head upon the pillow, I was almost afraid to go to sleep for fear that wonderful joy which came to us would not be there in the morning! But it has stayed with us through the years. God was so wonderful to us and has been always. He took away craving for drink immediately, and later gave us complete victory over other habits. He has blessed our home with a dear baby boy by adoption, and has done other wonderful things for us. As we have listened all these years, we have learned so much about the Bible and He has been able to use us in His service in our church. Since then we have seen our fathers and two brothers saved, and all four of them have gone home to glory.

We have a deep Christian love in our hearts for you both and we thank God every day for the Old-Fashioned Revival Hour.

❊　❊　❊

And one of the malefactors which were hanged railed on him, saying, If thou be Christ, save thyself and us.

135

But the other answering rebuked him, saying, Dost not thou fear God, seeing thou art in the same condemnation? And we indeed justly; for we receive the due reward of our deeds: but this man hath done nothing amiss. And he said unto Jesus, Lord, remember me when thou comest into thy kingdom (Luke 23:39–42).

Those who are familiar with the story of the founding of the Christian church will recall that dramatic midnight scene in Philippi (Acts 16) when a hardened Roman jailor got converted. There are some Christian jailors today. One of them writes from a prison in California.

Dear Mr. Fuller,

I am a guard and my work is in the prison hospital. It is here in the evening that some of the men listen to your Sunday night program and they are receiving a wonderful blessing from it. Most people think of a prison guard as one who is hard, cruel, and indifferent, but I am happy to say that here is one guard who, by the saving power of Jesus Christ, can still work in a prison and maintain a love in his heart for those who are incarcerated behind prison walls.

Heavenly Sunshine

The guard's conviction that the forgotten men behind bars are blessed by the Old-Fashioned Revival Hour is amply supported by letters to the Fullers written on the gray stationery of some of our largest penitentiaries.

Dear Sir,

    I heard your broadcast last Sunday and I can't find words to tell you how much I enjoyed to listen to it. I am trying to live a Christian life and broadcasts like yours help me more than I can say. I can't thank you enough for all that take part in the broadcast. I am in prison and will be for so many years that I don't like to count, but your broadcast helps me to do easier time and also makes my Bible much clearer and understandable. I may be wrong, but since I have turned to this life, I believe I have better eyesight. I now can read for hours without laying the Bible down. With your help on the broadcast and with our chaplain of this prison helping me, as long as the warden will let these broadcasts come in here, I can rest with the Lord. Some day, I too may be able to reach men and tell them about Christ. It is a wonderful feeling to be a Christian and know that your sins are all forgiven and you really can be happy, even in prison. May God bless you and the chaplain and all who have helped me so much.

Dear Rev. Fuller,

I am writing you to let you know how much your broadcast has helped me to come to know the Saviour and to feel His love. I found the Lord about a year ago and accepted Him after listening to one of your sermons. The lights are gone out here when you come on the air each Sunday night, but thank the Lord, there is a light to shine through my window from outside on a post, and it aids me in marking down the chapters and verses which you speak of. So the next morning I take my Bible and read the verses which you speak on and also meditate on them.

I am taking a Bible course in hopes that some day I may preach His Word and save souls. Being so far away from you, Rev. Fuller, did not change my mind about writing and letting you know that Christ has given me a joy and a peace of mind which the world couldn't give me, neither can the world take it away from me.

I have no people to help me or speak for me, since I have been in this trouble, as everyone seemed to turn their back on me; yet I haven't given up hope, as the Lord has been a father and mother to me here in prison and I am trusting Him to direct my paths. Please pray for me that I may grow strong in the Lord and keep His laws.

From Georgia comes this touching letter.

Dear Brother Fuller,

I am a young boy here in jail, sentenced to the electric chair, and I listen to your broadcast every Sunday and I sure do get lots of good from it. It sure makes me feel good when you tell me that God does forgive sin, and forgets them, too. I need to be forgiven. My father has turned against me in my troubles, so I have no one but God, and I know he will not foresake me.

I will listen to you every Sunday, just as long as I can. God bless you!

From Boston, on a postal card, a man writes:

Dear Dr. Fuller,

With the last two cents I have in the world, I purchased two postcards. One I have used to notify the authorities (who hold a warrant for me) as to my whereabouts, and the other one goes to you; you who is responsible for me seeing God's true light.

I have committed one of the most heinous crimes in the history of civil society, but your earnest, glorious and clear presentation of God's Word has seeped into my heart and forced my conscience to face the toll of the law. I am guilty.

You have shown me the way to forgiveness before God, and I have seen the light, and I want to pay for my crime and have my conscience clear. I shall do what is right. I thank you, and God bless you!

* * *

On our "itinerary of the soul in God," we have heard men and women from many lands and walks of life tell of what Christ has done for them through the Old-Fashioned Revival Hour. Charles E. Fuller, the founder and director of the broadcast, needs no other tribute than these letters; indeed none finer could be given him. It is not unfitting, however, that we should close our little volume with a word concerning him, especially since he never talks about himself. A lady from Kansas writes:

Dear Brother Fuller,

I have to tell you what a dear old colored lady said. My sister-in-law was talking in the grocery store and said, "I have a sister-in-law who likes to listen to the Old-Fashioned Revival Hour, and we do, too." And the colored lady said, throwing up her hands, "That Charles Fuller! THAT CHARLES FULLER! When he preaches, I gets such a blessing, I don't know whether I puts salt or soda in my biscuits."

Those who have heard Mr. Fuller preach, have heard one of the great preaching voices of our generation. It is said of the peerless George White-field, that he could say "Mesopotamia" so as to make men weep. Charles E. Fuller has something of that same power. As one young preacher wrote, "Brother Fuller's voice has *God* in it. It sounds

141

calm and sure in this day of fast living and quiets our lives." Sometimes, however, a man suits the ear better than the eye: Caruso's towering voice was in striking contrast to his modest stature. But in the case of Mr. Fuller, the many who have heard him are no more enthusiastic than the few who have seen him. A man writes, "You know, I shook hands with you once in Fort Worth, Texas, and I shall never forget that handshake—your big, kind, tender, strong, understanding hand." A woman in Texas went to hear Mr. Fuller preach and wrote of her encounter to a relative as follows:

Dear Ruth,

Monday night. Well, I don't know how to start this. I believe tonight I am the happiest woman in the world, or I would be, if only you could have been here. I met and shook hands with the beloved Brother Fuller. He is all and more than we expected him to be. He took his sermon from John 11:11, and did he preach! There were several saved, and several wanted to be prayed for. You know, I could hardly keep from crying as I sat there, hearing what I have wanted to hear and seeing what I have wanted to see for so long. I couldn't enjoy it thoroughly because you weren't there, and I knew you wanted to be there so bad.

Brother Fuller was supposed to get in at 3:30, and then he wasn't on that plane and another one came at 4:45, and naturally he was on that one. Everyone was looking for him. The station wagon drove up and out he and Rudy got, and he came in while everybody was singing "Heavenly Sunshine." Everybody stood up. Hot, gosh, it was 106! He said he expected to get a big welcome, but not such a warm welcome.

Do you know the first thing he did? He gathered all the children from 15 years old down around him on the platform and they sang "Heavenly Sunshine." He told them he wanted them to be able to say they had sung with the famous pianist Rudy Atwood. The song they sang at the end of his sermon was, "Meet Me There." I could talk or write a year and not be able to tell you all about how wonderful it was. It was so late when they got through that the sun was down. By the way, I was sitting in the second seat and I had a good view of everything. I got to shake hands with Mr. Fuller, too. Goodness, he's a big man, and he has big hands, too, and he shakes your hand as though he was glad to.

Tuesday night. Well, I thought yesterday was the happiest day of my life, but no, definitely NO! Tonight we went over to Dallas to the bandstand to hear Brother Fuller. But I will begin at this morning. I got up and from the minute my feet touched the floor everything went like clockwork; my washing, ironing, dinner, and everything. We got off so easy to hear Brother Fuller, and the most wonderful sermon I ever heard. He asked who wanted to be prayed for, and Jack [her husband] held up his hand, honest he did! They gave the invitation and down he run; what I mean, he hardly touched the floor! And then the sweetest thing happened. In among those hundreds and hundreds of people Brother Roper saw Jack coming down the aisle, and he come up the aisle to meet him. I saw him loving him and patting him, but I didn't know until later that he didn't say one word to Jack. He told me he couldn't, he was crying so hard. He told me he told his wife, if there was no one saved but Jack it would be well worth the trip for Brother Fuller. He told me he and his wife had gone on their knees and prayed so earnestly for him. You tell me he's not our friend! You talk about somebody being gloriously saved. Jack was! I have never seen anything like it, and there was so many more, too! God certainly answers prayer! Now I must stop. It is 1:20 o'clock. I know you are happy for us. The old sow and pigs are doing fine.

144

On January 9, 1955, Dr. Fuller was privileged, in the providence of God, to celebrate the thirtieth anniversary of the Old-Fashioned Revival Hour. Letters from all over the world were received, such as the following from England.

Dear Reverend Fuller,

Last night from eleven to twelve I listened to the most delightful broadcast that ever was, for I felt God's presence so keenly. My face was wet with tears most of the hour, because I was so overjoyed and happy for Dr. Fuller on his thirtieth anniversary. How I love him! I have only been listening to the Old-Fashioned Revival Hour for about six years, but what blessings I have received in that time! Dear Mrs. Fuller, will you thank Mr. Fuller for me? I love Dan's prayers, too, and oh, how I love the music. And hearing about the flowers today there in the auditorium. Mine were tears of joy mostly, but there were some sad tears, because I always have to listen alone, as my husband and his sister, who lives with us, are not interested in any religious programs and I cannot get my other relatives to listen either. Isn't that sad? Christ is such a wonderful Saviour, and they need Him as their Saviour, too. I have been a Christian for over forty years. Thank you for all the heavenly sunshine you bring us.

As Moses longed to see the Promised Land, so many have dreamed of the day when they might visit a live broadcast of the Old-Fashioned Revival Hour. After each broadcast, those present for the first time queue up at the front of the auditorium to shake hands with us. Many listeners, realizing this to be an unattainable dream, solace themselves with the hope of shaking Brother Fuller's hand in glory, though making it very plain that to visit the broadcast would be a little bit of heaven. At the time of the thirtieth anniversary celebration in Long Beach, something happened in this regard as charming to the fancy as anything in the Arabian Nights, but laden with the pathos of real life. Going back to pick up the thread of our story, it all began one day when a poor farmer in Cimarron (population 1,189), Kansas, sat down and diffidently inscribed the following letter.

Dear Rev. and Mrs. Fuller,

I have listened for years and have received unmeasurable riches from your program, but have failed to write in and have been able to send little or nothing to help out. I first started listening when we got our first radio back in 1937 during the dust storm years. We were living on the old farm for sixteen years and we only raised three wheat crops in all that time. I lost the old farm, but somehow God helped me and the good wife and we raised up four children to man and womanhood, that they might go out into this world with a college education; something I never had.

Well, Reverend Fuller, it would take me hours to tell you what I think of your program and what it meant to us during those discouraging years to have the Old-Fashioned Revival Hour come into our home every Sunday, when you would tell us to put our trust in God and He never would fail us. How it did comfort us! I must close now, as I'm very poor at writing and there are so many that are better at expressing themselves than I am, but I want to tell you a little bit more.

I have a dear, good wife and a fifth child, a boy, thirteen years old, at home. I am out of work and older, and it's hard to get work because everywhere they want younger men. The Lord wants us older men for Him, though, and I'm so thankful He never says, "You are too old." I hope to live to hear your granddaughter sing with you some day. How wonderful for father and son to be working together for Christ. I have prayed for your organization for many years, and I do hope and pray the Lord will call one of my boys, if not all of them, into His service. Please excuse my mistakes in this long letter. I would feel that I were very near heaven's door if I could visit one of your programs and shake your hand, Reverend Fuller.

A party in Des Moines, Iowa, heard the above letter read and called TWA officials, suggesting that they fly the man from Kansas to the anniversary broadcast in Long Beach, California. The good folk TWA outdid themselves in acquiescence, providing not only transportation, but de luxe entertainment for the party concerned. On Christmas day, 1955, in the same little town of Cimarron, Kansas, a second letter was written.

Dear Rev. and Mrs. Fuller,

Never in my life was I at such a loss for words as I am tonight. I was sitting in our small front room with my good wife and son, with less than one dollar in my pocket. I had gotten a small gift for my wife, but had to explain to my thirteen-year-old son that I would have to get him something later. Then the

phone rang, and a Mr. Cy Jackson called by
long distance from Des Moines, stating that I
was selected to be flown by TWA to your most
wonderful anniversary program on January
9th. [Mr. Jackson is public relations coordinator for the Gospel Broadcasting Association.
It was he who gave the TWA people their
bright idea.] My dear brother, Reverend Fuller, I never expected to meet you this side of
our dear Christ's eternal home for us believers.
Reverend Fuller, I feel so unworthy to be selected to come to be on your wonderful program. I sure was astonished, like the shepherds
who were tending their flocks some nineteen
hundred years ago this Christmas season. I will
never be able to express my appreciation of
such a wonderful blessing happening in my
whole life. I have been putting off and putting
off writing you, Reverend Fuller, ever since I
heard my letter read over the air on your program. My son and I were visiting that Sunday
afternoon, last November 14th, both talking
quietly and listening to the wonderful music
from your program, when Mrs. Fuller began
reading that letter from the man from Kansas.
My boy looked at me and said, "Why, Dad,
that's *your* letter that Mrs. Fuller is reading."
And there was a mighty astonished father and
son looking at each other with a happiness

that I will never forget. I haven't written sooner, Brother Fuller, because I've been out of work most of the time and it has been so hard making ends meet. I did want to acknowledge the reading of my letter over the air with at least a small offering for the Lord's work, but I just haven't had it. I know you will understand. There are so many men out of work here and the farmers are hard up, too, as crops have been very poor this year.

Well, Brother Fuller, since I have been invited and the Lord willing, I feel so happy that I'll be able to see all of the people on your Old-Fashioned Revival Hour very soon. I certainly thank our loving Lord. As the good old gospel song says, "I have joy unspeakable," till I'll be shaking your hand in Long Beach, California, soon. What a wonderful Christmas you have made for me!

Once more, from Cimarron, Kansas:

Dear Dr. Fuller,

I just don't know how to express myself to you and Mrs. Fuller and all the Old-Fashioned Revival Hour people, who made my trip to California the most outstanding event of my whole life. I arrived back home in Cimarron last Sunday night. I found my wife and son very well and everything here at home as usual.

The air trip was very enjoyable. I spent Sunday with some wonderful, spiritual friends in Kansas City. I will be glad when Sunday comes again so that I can listen to your program as usual. Give my Christian love to all now, as I am a seven-day-a-week salesman for the Old-Fashioned Revival Hour. As soon as I can find work, I want to get six or seven of the books, *The Tabernacle in the Wilderness,* to pass out to my preacher friends back here. But work is very scarce and I am not sure when I will get work.

Give my fondest Christian regards to Mrs. Fuller. May the Lord bless you always.

The anniversary was a milestone, but not the end. Never weary in well doing, with thirty years behind him, Charles Fuller is still lowering the gospel net and bringing up new fishes. Two recent letters are typical.

My dear Dr. Fuller,

So many miles separate us, you and I, that you cannot see my hand held high, asking you

to pray for me. I have this moment turned off
my radio, having heard your wonderful broadcast for the first time. I am moved to tears, for,
at thirty-eight years of age, I now know what
it is that I have so long yearned for: the Word
of God. Doctor Fuller, you have found me.
Pray for me, please, for I am a sinner. I am a
lonely soul, not knowing what I have wanted
all these years, but now your voice and the
voice of your dear wife and friends giving the
music; oh, why did I not hear you before!

Thirty years you have sent out your message
of hope and I did not know. I shall pray tonight that the Lord in His goodness will direct
me. Are you on at other times? Pray for me,
dear Doctor Fuller, and write and tell me that
you have received this letter.

A letter from Lancashire, England:

Dear Dr. Fuller,

I lost my dear wife in July of 1954, and I
now live on my own, as our family of five are
all married, and ever since my great loss I have
been very lonely and depressed. I am sure my
prayers to Almighty God have been answered,
and part of it is that I found your broadcast on

February 10, 1955, near midnight. I was just
going to bed and something, which is beyond
words to explain, caused me to turn on the
wireless, and I had the surprise of my life when
I found that this was your thirtieth year of
broadcasting. And to think that all these years
have gone by in my life and I have never heard
of you or your work! I must admit I am
ashamed of myself. I have talked about this
experience of finding your blessed broadcast
while at work, and all the men with whom I
work seem to be so interested. I have always
had faith in God, but I have never before ex-
ercised that faith, and have never had the joy
of being born again into God's family. Oh, it
is wonderful! I am sixty-three years old, and I
don't believe that I will ever miss another one
of your broadcasts, for through hearing you I
have found Christ as my Saviour.

We conclude with the greeting given by Mr. Fuller
to his radio audience on the occasion of the thirtieth anniversary broadcast.

My loving, dear friends of the Old-Fashioned
Revival Hour,

Some of you are new friends and some have been listening for various lengths of time, up to thirty years. Just think of that! My, what God has done! It is a miracle that He should permit this broadcast to grow from one small station to hundreds of radio stations so that this troubled old world could be given hope, and blanketed for so many years with the glorious gospel of our Lord Jesus Christ.

The messages have been simple, for I am not a gifted speaker; but they have been true to the Word of God, the old Book, God's Book, so that the Holy Spirit could empower them. And always I have loved the souls of men. I expect some day to meet in the glory land hosts of men and women and children redeemed by the blood of the lamb, who are there in heaven because, listening to the radio, they have heard that God loves them and offers them the free gift of salvation. Yes, they will be there from every country on the globe. Some have heard in their homes, some in their cars, in hospitals, on ships at sea, in prison, in cocktail lounges, in Arctic snows and steaming jungles, and in Army camps. Yes, God has touched hearts the world over through the beloved Old-Fashioned Revival Hour.

I am so thankful I have such a faithful helpmate in Mrs. Fuller, "Honey" to me, who reads bits from your letters on each broadcast. I am also deeply grateful for the consecrated musicians: Mr. Leland Green, who directs the chorus of lovely singers, for the quartet and Rudy at the piano and George Broadbent at the organ. Many of you have written that we have heavenly music on the program, and that is the way I feel about it, too.

Thank you, friends, for your prayers, for your support through the years, and may God richly bless each one of you.

*   *   *

And now, good reader, you have read our little book. We hope you have found more there than an interesting variety of religious experience; that you have been able to see that the gospel is indeed the "power of God unto salvation." The Scriptures say, ". . . as many as received him, to them gave he power to become the sons of God . . ." (John 1:12). Have you received Christ as He is freely offered to you in the gospel? If not, you cannot plead ignorance, for we have called before you a host of witnesses from all parts of the world and from all walks of life, and they have borne to you a clear testimony of the saving power of Jesus Christ. Do not presume upon time, for not only must you die *some* time, you may die *any* time. The only time of which you can be sure is the present. Why not take your stand *now* with those whose good confession you have just read? ". . . behold, *now* is the accepted time; behold, *now* is the day of salvation" (II Corinthians 6:2).